GREAT BRITISH
Shipwrecks
A Personal Adventure

Rod Macdonald

Whittles Publishing

Published by
Whittles Publishing Ltd.,
Dunbeath,
Caithness, KW6 6EG,
Scotland, UK

www.whittlespublishing.com

ISBN 978-184995-077-0

Also by Rod Macdonald:

Dive Scapa Flow
Dive Scotland's Greatest Wrecks
Dive England's Greatest Wrecks
Into the Abyss: Diving to Adventure in the Liquid World
The Darkness Below

www.rod-macdonald.co.uk

www.authorsplace.co.uk/rod-macdonald

www.amazon.com/author/rodmacdonald

Cover image courtesy of Barry McGill www.deepwreckexplorers.com

Printed by Cambrian Printers

CONTENTS

ACKNOWLEDGEMENTS

To dive alone is to die alone. It's one of the common phrases bandied about in diving circles – and is undeniably true. To try and avoid that fate, divers tend to dive in buddy pairs, each looking after the other as best we can down there. To all those divers – too many to mention individually – who have accompanied me on survey dives and put up with me haring round a shipwreck on a personal mission, my grateful thanks. Thanks also to the many skippers around the UK who have gone out of their way to get me to where I needed to go.

Thanks are also due to the following contributors:

Rob Ward of Illusion Illustration, Bridge of Muchalls, Aberdeenshire; creator of all the wonderful shipwreck illustrations in this book over the course of the last 25 years or so. *www.illusionillustration.co.uk*

Ewan Rowell, legend of Scottish diving and closed circuit rebreathers and my regular dive buddy on many of the wrecks in this book from 1989 until a move to Oz a few years ago, for allowing me to use some of his underwater photos.

My present-day regular dive buddies, Greg Booth, Jim Burke, Richard Colliar, Paul Haynes, Gary Petrie and Tony Ray, for the adventures, support and assistance (and general mick taking) they have offered.

Bob Anderson, skipper of the MV *Halton* in Scapa Flow for casting his canny eye over my new Scapa Flow wreck illustrations and for use of some of his underwater photos. *www.mvhalton.co.uk*

Ben Wade of Scapa Scuba, Stromness, for his help with the new Scapa Flow illustrations. *www.scapascuba.co.uk*

Grainne Patton for allowing me to use (again!) her wonderful photo of the boilers on SS *Empire Heritage* and her haunting image of HMS *Audacious*.

Steve Collard, who accompanied me on all the English Channel shipwreck dives.

Bob Macpherson, ex-crewman on the *Empire Chief*, who gave me his World War II account of his crew's night out with the *Empire Heritage* crew in Hoboken, New York, the night before *Empire Heritage* set off for the UK on what would be her final fatal voyage.

Ian Williamson for preparing the location charts.

Barry McGill of Ireland and Deep Wreck Explorers, for his assistance and for allowing me to use his wonderful photos of the *Justicia*, HMS *Audacious* and SS *Empire Heritage*. The stunning cover shot of the gun turret on HMS *Audacious* is his. *www.deepwreckexplorers.com*

Ian Lawler and Stewart Andrews for their constructive comments on my illustrations of HMS *Audacious*, SS *Empire Heritage* and *Justicia*.

Stevie Adams, Ross Coventry and Shane Wasik for their assistance with the section on HMS *Pathfinder*.

Dougall Campbell for his thoughts on the remains of HMS *Audacious*.

INTRODUCTION

Great **British Shipwrecks** focuses on 37 of the most well-known shipwrecks around the UK, providing for each a narrative of the ship's history, its demise and condition today and an artist's illustration of the wreck on the seabed. It has taken a personal underwater journey of more than 30 years diving to get into the position of being able to put all this information into one book.

As a 21-year-old, newly qualified diver, when I first towed my beloved 5-metre squidgy inflatable dive boat up to Scapa Flow in 1981 to dive the legendary scuttled German High Seas Fleet wrecks from World War I, I was surprised to find that there was virtually no information on the wrecks available for the visiting diver. There were no diver-orientated books, there was no Internet teeming with information; there was nothing – and worse still, the wrecks themselves were not buoyed. When we arrived, we looked out forlornly across Scapa Flow and just saw a vast and empty 12-mile expanse of black and foreboding water.

We had to find the wrecks the old way: by taking bearings to land points from the wreck symbols marked on the Admiralty Chart. After applying variation to the bearings, we motored my squidgy out to the approximate position for the wreck in the middle of the Flow, using a hand compass to check our charted land bearings and close in on the target wreck as best we could. There were no cheap digital echo sounders available on the market then (as today), which would easily reveal the wreck on the bottom – so to finally find the German ships, we dropped our anchor and trawled up and down the Flow dragging it

Salvage diver working on the scuttled German Fleet.
Orkney Library. William Hourston Collection

in 1990 and now in its 4th edition).

Once I had come up with the idea of writing a diver guide to the Scapa Flow wrecks, I decided to illustrate each of the main shipwrecks and provide an overview of the wreck at a glance. I invited several artists to pitch for the job of illustrating the wrecks, which would be based on topside photos, underwater photos and my own humble scratching's made on waterproof notepads as I swam round the wrecks. One artist stood out head and shoulders above the others: Rob Ward of Illusion Illustration – who coincidentally lives just about 5 miles away from me. Rob is a very talented and precise artist who is as equally at home illustrating wildlife and creating portraits as he is illustrating new houses for sales brochures or illustrating an underwater ROV (remotely-operated vehicle) for an offshore oil company. He has illustrated many other books.

Rob's illustrations of the German wrecks for *Dive Scapa Flow* were the first time anyone had attempted to seriously illustrate these

The wreck of the light cruiser SMS Dresden *at Scapa Flow with, inset, how she looked in 1989. Note the difference at the foredeck* © Rod Macdonald

behind on the bottom until we snagged ourselves a German battleship – like an old wire-sweep from yesteryear. Even then, as we got ready to dive we didn't know which particular wreck we were diving – whether it was a battleship or light cruiser, whether it was sitting upright on its keel, laying on its side or completely upside down. Each first dive was a voyage of discovery, but gradually we could build up a picture of each wreck. This interest in shipwrecks, and the obvious dearth of diver information for the historic wrecks at Scapa Flow, led to my first book, *Dive Scapa Flow* (first published by Mainstream Publishing, Edinburgh

wrecks – and over the years, divers have given me much positive feedback, as they used them to plan dives and understand the wreck in advance. Any inaccuracies in the illustrations are mine alone – as Rob is not a diver and has never seen the wrecks.

I was given six months to research, dive, and write the manuscript for *Dive Scapa Flow* – and so I spent as much time as possible up in Orkney, frantically swimming round all of these huge wrecks and noting them as best as I could. Of course, there were things that I missed – such as when I was back home finalising the image of the light cruiser *Dresden* and I realised that there was a large section midships that I hadn't noted properly. The skipper I was using at the time in Orkney, Keith Thomson, kindly took the local Kirkwall dive club out on a free evening's dive so they could survey the missing section for me. It was also helpful latterly to be put in touch with Dougall Campbell, whose company Scapa Flow Salvage Co. Ltd, owned the German wrecks in the 1970s and salved the armour belts from the German battleships. Despite many decades passing since he worked in Scapa Flow, Dougall still has a forensic knowledge of where the blasting took place and was able to look over my images and correct them as appropriate.

But, no sooner had I published these illustrations than I realised the speed at which the wrecks were decaying and falling apart – rendering them out of date almost immediately. Throughout the following years, as reprints and subsequent editions of the book took place, I corrected the illustrations when I could. The rate of decay and collapse however,

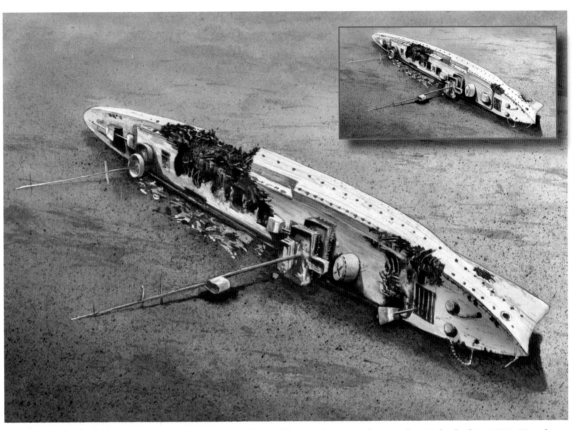

The wreck of the light cruiser SMS Brummer *at Scapa Flow with, inset, the wreck as it looked in 1989. Note how the foredeck 5.9-inch gun has fallen from its mount to the seabed* © Rod Macdonald

is accelerating – almost exponentially – and eventually significant changes had to be made to the original images. As an example, opposite are two images of the *Dresden*. The main image is the 2007 (4th edition) version. The inset image is the 1989, 1st edition image. Differential corrosion had been at work since she sank in 1919, turning the rivets that held the main foredeck to the hull, to dust. In about 1995, a small gap opened up at the join of the deck to the uppermost starboard side of the hull. Then, slowly but inexorably over the coming years, the deck fell outwards and downwards to expose the whole innards of the bow section.

Likewise, above are two illustrations of the wreck of the light cruiser *Brummer*. The main illustration is the 2007, 4th edition version and the inset image is the 1989, 1st edition image. The 2007 (4th edition) image shows how the foredeck 5.9-inch gun has fallen from its mount to the seabed, pulling some of the foredeck with it. Over the last year or two the whole bridge superstructure and foredeck in front of it has now collapsed down so this illustration will be updated when it comes to a 5th edition.

In 1993, my second book, *Dive Scotland's Greatest Wrecks*, was published, covering 14 of the most well-known shipwrecks around Scotland – and again, I called on Rob Ward's services to illustrate each. Then, in 2003, *Dive England's Greatest Wrecks* was published, covering ten of the most famous English shipwrecks – Rob, again, illustrated each one for me.

The shipwreck illustrations Rob has prepared for me over the years form a snapshot of a small part of Britain's maritime past and I always felt that the illustrations were important in their own right – so I determined to bring all these images together and also commission new work from Rob. It's fair to say that he has been hard at work for me over the last few months as we created many new images – such as of the battleship *König*, the *Bayern* turrets, the trawler *James Barrie*, HMS *Pathfinder*, RMS *Justicia*, HMS *Audacious*, SS *Empire Heritage* and others.

Rob and I have developed a process for preparing each image, which is by necessity quite time consuming. Initially I have to physically get to the shipwreck, dive it several times and survey it. I then prepare a file for Rob, giving him topside photos of the ship afloat and as much subsea information as possible in advance of a brain-storming meeting where I try to convey to him the way the ship lies. Rob picks it up very quickly and we have developed an understanding over the years, as he patiently, and sometimes with a wry smile, lets me sketch (as would a child in primary school) how the wreck lies, before he takes over and starts deftly kicking things into shape. Rob also researches the ship himself and very soon we have a working draft image that we can tweak and improve upon.

Once these images are published in a book, that's it until a new edition comes out, when I get the opportunity of making amendments to take into account any significant recent changes. The images are not, and cannot be, updated every year: they are a snapshot in time of the wreck when it was illustrated – and things may well have changed significantly since that time.

We also have to take a view on how best to represent the wreck to show divers the salient parts. The images are artist's illustrations – not photographs – and are designed to illustrate for divers what they can expect to see. Were it possible to photograph or put a multibeam image of the whole wreck on a single page in a book, then lots of features would simply be too small to be seen. Thus, the German light cruisers at Scapa Flow are long and sleek, but to get a useful illustration of them on a single page we have had to compress and fatten them up a bit. We also have to make important features, like guns or capstans slightly larger than they are in reality, so divers can see them in the illustrations. If it was all done exactly according to scale, many features would never be seen.

So, here is a collection of all these illustrations – old and new, seen and never before seen – of some of the most loved and visited shipwrecks around the UK. These wrecks are the ones that drew me to them during the course of my own diving career and so this book is really the result of my own haphazard personal wreck diving adventure. Whilst some wrecks are obvious for inclusion, others are perhaps more esoteric and out of the way. For example, HMS *Pathfinder*, a technical dive in the Firth of Forth, is not a name that is on every diver's lips – but she is important because she was the first Royal Naval warship to be sunk by a torpedo fired from a German U-boat in World War I.

I have also not confined myself to wrecks in the air-diving range, but have incorporated wrecks that are firmly in the realm of today's technical diver using mixed diving gases such as Trimix.

Hopefully, most divers will see some wrecks that they have personally visited, but will also find others of interest that they have never seen. I also hope that this book will appeal to non-divers alike; to folk simply interested in the sea and the mysteries it holds.

Rod Macdonald
2012

1

ORKNEY & SCAPA FLOW

21 June 1919 – the German High Seas Fleet scuttles at Scapa Flow

Scapa Flow, the great natural deep-water harbour some 12 miles across and almost completely encircled by the Orkney Islands, hosts the largest easily accessible collection of German World War I shipwrecks in the world. It has justly become one of the world's top dive locations and each year thousands of divers journey to Scapa Flow to explore the three massive German battleships and four light cruisers that rest there – as well as to dive the countless other shipwrecks that lie in the depths of the Flow. But it is undoubtedly the remaining naval wrecks of the once powerful German High Seas Fleet that are the main attraction.

As a condition of the Armistice of 11 November 1918 – which suspended the hostilities of World War I pending the negotiation of the Treaty of Versailles – the 74 warships of the German Imperial Navy's High Seas Fleet were to be interned under British guard at Scapa Flow. The High Seas Fleet had survived the war relatively intact and could still pose a very real threat to the Allies if the Armistice broke down and the fighting restarted. Therefore, as a condition of the Armistice, the German Fleet would be interned at Scapa Flow under the close guard of the British. The High Seas Fleet was effectively to be held hostage during the peace negotiations. The First

The German High Sea Fleet at anchor in Scapa Flow in 1919. Courtesy Orkney Library. Tom Kent Collection

Battle Squadron of the British Grand Fleet – commanded by Sir Sydney Fremantle and consisting of five battleships, two light cruisers and nine destroyers – was stationed at Scapa Flow and would keep a watchful eye on the Germans.

The 74 ships of the German Fleet consisted of five massive battlecruisers, eleven battleships, eight cruisers and fifty torpedo-boat destroyers.

After crossing from their German bases, the High Seas Fleet rendezvoused with the British Grand Fleet at a pre-arranged location in the North Sea. There were a combined 90,000 men afloat on 370 warships – no such massive sea force had ever been assembled before. The German warships had been ordered to have their guns disarmed before they left Germany and should have no longer been a threat to the British vessels, but the British were taking no chances of any German treachery: their guns were loaded and the crews at action stations alertly looking for any signs of trouble.

The British Fleet split into two lines of battleships and battlecruisers, six miles apart and stretching out of sight into the distance. The German Fleet sailed into the middle of this passage of steel in single column and was escorted to Scapa Flow.

On a cold November day in 1918 the two Fleets arrived at Scapa Flow, the German ships mooring in neat rows. The bulk of the crews who had sailed the fleet over – some 20,000 sailors – were then repatriated to Germany, leaving only skeleton care-taking crews aboard who were confined to their ships and not allowed ashore.

The peace negotiations dragged on from November 1918 throughout the winter of 1918/19, through Easter 1919 and then into the early summer. The once proud light-grey warships of the German Fleet slowly became streaked with surface rust and marine growth from their long stay at anchor.

At the very beginning of the Armistice talks, the Allies insisted that the Germans would be responsible for supplying their own fleet whilst it was in internment. The British would provide only water, coal and oil – as they recognised the insurmountable difficulties that supplying these essentials from Germany would entail. The Germans were also given four-day-old newspapers by the British – in the belief that nothing sensitive could be gleaned from them. However, these old papers were avidly read as they were one of the few means the Germans had of keeping up with what was going on in the outside world. The German sailors were not allowed ashore and so could not obtain any information from local sources. In addition, all German wireless receivers had been collected and taken away by the British.

After seven long months of internment, on 20 June 1919, Rear Admiral Ludwig von Reuter, in command of the German Fleet, read in the latest four-day-old newspaper, *The Times* of 16 June, of the German counter-proposals to the latest Allied peace terms. He then read in *The Times* of 17 June of the Allied refusal to accept any of the German counter-proposals. The Germans were given five days to accept the position, failing which the Allies declared that a state of war would exist again.

From the brusque tone of the speeches reported in *The Times*, it seemed to von Reuter that there was little chance of a peace deal being agreed – and that the Armistice would likely end on 21 June. If so, von Reuter suspected that the British would immediately seize his fleet. With only skeleton crews aboard and all guns disarmed, he would be incapable of stopping the seizure. The Armistice had in fact been extended by two days, to 7 p.m. on Monday 23 June – but after the scuttling, von Reuter claimed he had not been advised of this; the British counter-claimed that he had been told. The jury is still out on that one. With von Reuter apparently believing that war would restart, the die was cast for 21 June 1919. It would be an historic day – one that still affects the daily lives of Orcadian folk.

At 9 a.m., the British Grand Fleet Squadron left Scapa Flow for the first time in the seven long months of internment, to carry out a long-range torpedo-firing exercise at sea, safe in the knowledge that the Armistice had been extended for two days. A small guard-force of three British destroyers – *Vegar*, *Vesper* and an unserviceable destroyer, *Victorious*, were left behind.

At 10 a.m., Rear Admiral Ludwig von Reuter appeared in full dress-uniform on the quarterdeck of his flagship, the cruiser *Emden*. He wore the insignia of his highest decorations around his neck and his Iron Cross and other medals were pinned to the breast of his coat. He paced up and down the quarterdeck, stopping frequently to study the other ships of the fleet through his telescope. One of his staff advised him that the British warships on guard-duty had left the Flow with their supporting cruisers and destroyers on an exercise earlier that morning. Von Reuter could hardly believe his luck. He ordered the international code flag 'DG' to be raised on *Emden*. This signal alerted the officers of his other ships to man their bridges and keep a special lookout for further signals.

At 10.30 a.m. a string of command flags appeared over *Emden*, even though this was well outwith the set times permitted by the British for issuing signals. The order read: '*PARAGRAPH 11. BESTÄTIGEN*' – 'Paragraph 11. Confirm.' The pre-arranged coded order to the commanders of the other ships in the fleet to scuttle their vessels had just been given. Unbeknown to the British, for the last four days Reuter's trusted sailors had been securing doors and hatches in the open position – some were welded open – so that the ships could flood more easily. Seacocks had been set on a hair-turning and lubricated thoroughly. Large hammers had been placed beside any valves that would allow water to flood in if knocked off and bulkhead rivets had been prised out. Now that the order to scuttle had been given, seacocks were opened and disconnected from the upper deck, to prevent the British closing them if they boarded before the ship went under. Seawater pipes were smashed and condensers opened. As valves and seacocks were opened, their keys and handles were thrown overboard so that they could never be closed again. Once the vessels started to scuttle, there was no way to stop the ship sinking, other than by taking it in tow and beaching it.

The signal to scuttle was repeated from ship to ship by semaphore and by Morse code on signal lamps, and travelled slowly around the fleet. The southernmost ships of the long lines of torpedo boat destroyers were not visible from the flagship *Emden* and it took a full hour before the order reached them. The pre-arranged formal responses came back, slowly to begin with. The first reached *Emden* at about 11.30 a.m., just as the original

The battleship Bayern *sinking. C. W. Burrows*

signal to scuttle reached the last of the destroyers: 'PARAGRAPH ELEVEN IS CONFIRMED.'

In a patriotic gesture of defiance, many of the German ships ran up the Imperial Navy ensign at their sterns. The prohibited white flag with its bold black cross and eagle had not been seen at Scapa Flow before. Others ran up the red flag, the letter 'Z', which in international code signaled: 'Advance on the enemy.'

At noon, an artist who had hitched a ride on one of the patrolling Royal Navy trawlers to sketch the German Fleet at anchor, noticed that small boats were being lowered down the side of some of the German ships against British standing orders. He advised a British officer, but only 16 minutes later, the first of the warships to sink, the *Friedrich der Grosse*, turned turtle and went to the bottom.

Some of the warships sank on an even keel, whilst others rolled slowly onto their sides. Some went down by the bow or stern, forcing the other end of the ship to lift high out of the water. The top-heavy battleships moored in deeper water turned turtle on the surface before sinking. Those ships moored in shallower water settled onto the seabed, leaving their masts and funnels standing proud of the water. Blasts of steam, oil and air roared out of vents and white clouds of vapour billowed up from the sides of the ships. Great anchor chains snapped with the strain and crashed into the sea or whiplashed against the decks and sides of the ships. The ships groaned and protested as they were subjected to stresses and strains for which they had never been designed. Von Reuter's own ship *Emden* was one of the last to start scuttling, because two British drifters and a water supply vessel were alongside delivering stores and water.

As each vessel passed from sight, a whirlpool was created. Debris swirled around in it, slowly being sucked inwards and eventually being pulled under into the murky depths. Gradually, oil escaping from submerged ships spread upwards and outwards to cover the surface of the sea with a dark film. Scattered across the Flow were lifeboats, hammocks, lifebelts, chests, spars, gratings and all the debris of a ship's passing.

Hundreds of German sailors abandoned their ships into lifeboats. On one of the largest warships, sailors lined up on the deck and cheered a farewell to another ship close by as it slid beneath the waves. One German sailor was seen dancing a hornpipe on the deck of the *Baden*.

When it was initially ascertained that the entire German High Seas Fleet had started to scuttle, the small British guard-force quickly realised the enormity of what was being done and how impotent they were to stop it. The two British destroyers *Vegar* and *Vesper* steamed into the channel between the islands of Hoy and Fara towards the tail end of the ranks of moored torpedo-boats. They opened fire as they closed, with small arms, machine-guns and larger guns. Three Germans in a lifeboat containing 13 men were killed and four were wounded. The others were ordered back on board their ship and forced by threats of further shooting to turn off the flood valves. A stoker in the lifeboat of *V 127* was shot in the stomach and died shortly afterwards. A British drifter was seen towing two or three lifeboats full of German sailors. One of them stood up and tried to cut his boat free from the towrope. A Royal Marine raised his rifle and shot him dead.

A British drifter put an armed boarding-party aboard the battleship *Markgraf*. The captain, Lt-Cdr Walther Schumann, delayed as long as he could before emerging to meet the boarding-party, waving a white flag. He refused to obey an order from the boarding-party to order his own men to go below and shut off the flood valves – or to allow the Royal Navy boarding-party to do so. The boarding-party attempted to halt the scuttle and a scuffle broke out in which Schumann was shot through the head and died immediately. Another officer was seriously wounded, but enough had been done to ensure *Markgraf* went to the bottom. In all, the British managed to beach three ships of the 50 ships in the torpedo-boat flotilla. Five others sank in shallow waters and remained visible, with their superstructure standing proud of the water.

Scapa Flow echoed to the sound of gunfire from British vessels – but shots also came from the land, as British troops and locals alike repelled lifeboats filled with German sailors seeking to land on the shore. On the island of Cava a group of women wielding pitchforks and other farm-tools managed to scare off a lifeboat with a party of Germans who were trying to land on the beach. In total, nine German sailors died that day and 16 were wounded.

At 2 p.m. the British First Battle Squadron of the Grand Fleet returned from their aborted exercise and steamed at full speed into the Flow. The massive British warships surged through the water at 22 knots, smashing through the short seas of Scapa Flow in a spectacle of power and aggression. One Royal Navy destroyer broke off from the main group and cut the sinking *Emden*'s anchor-cable before successfully towing her to the shore where she was beached. Some Royal Navy destroyers also fired warning salvoes of shells from their main guns. Armed boarding-parties went aboard the battleship *Baden* where they managed to restart the diesel generation units, restoring power and lighting and enabling systematic pumping to start.

The commander of the British destroyer group threatened any German commander whose ship sank with summary execution – and a number of German officers were lined up by the British on the torpedo-boat destroyer

S 132. A Royal Marine firing squad was drawn up, but no executions took place. A man described in contemporary accounts as 'an English sailor', but probably an off-duty officer who had hastily returned to his ship from ashore, boarded another German destroyer and put a pistol to the head of a German officer. He pulled the trigger – and missed. In the heat of the moment, the barrel had slipped and the officer survived with a bad cut, muzzle-blast burns and a loud ringing in his ears.

In addition to beaching the *Emden*, the scuttling of two other light cruisers was also thwarted. The *Frankfurt* was beached just as the waters of the Flow began to wash over her decks and the *Nürnberg* was also taken in tow and run aground after a British destroyer had severed her anchor-chain with explosives. The drifter *Clonsin* took another light cruiser, *Dresden*, in tow - even though she was so low in the water that her main deck was awash. Painfully slowly, the *Clonsin* made for the beach on the island of Cava less than a mile away. On the way, *Dresden* lurched down by the head and then capsized and sank so quickly that there was no time to cast off the tow-cable.

On the 24,610-ton battlecruiser *Seydlitz*, the entire crew stood proudly to attention on the deck, singing the German national anthem and watching as the 22,640-ton battlecruiser *Moltke* sank beside them. They then had to abandon their own ship and 40 minutes later the *Seydlitz* followed the *Moltke* to the bottom.

Von Reuter himself was taken aboard HMS *Revenge* where a short and bitter exchange took place between him and Sir Sydney Fremantle, who was in charge of the British Fleet. Von Reuter tried to explain that he had given the order to scuttle because he genuinely believed that the Armistice was to end that day and that hostilities were about to recommence. Von Reuter claimed to be amazed when he was told that the Armistice had been extended by two days. Fremantle subsequently always maintained that he had informed von Reuter 'unofficially' of the extension, before the scuttling. Von Reuter for his part always denied having any knowledge of the extension prior to the evening of 21 June 1919.

The scuttled German destroyer G102. *C.W. Burrows*

The drifter Ramna *stranded on the submerged hull of the battlecruiser* Moltke. *C.W. Burrows*

That night, British warships laden with the 1,744 homeless German officers and men, set off southwards from Orkney bound for Nigg in the Cromarty Firth. At Nigg, the Germans were handed over from naval custody into military custody and from there were then moved southwards by train to prisoner-of-war camps in the north of England.

Whilst the British Press reaction was hostile, the German Press acclaimed the scuttling as the last heroic act of the German Navy. Von Reuter managed to get his explanation for the scuttling out of his POW camp in England to his superiors in Germany by having an officer who was due to be repatriated memorise it for subsequent repetition to the German command on his return. The officer's repatriation was unfortunately delayed and he was only able to pass on the message in mid-August.

The British Admiralty subsequently attempted on two occasions to bring von Reuter to trial, but on both occasions the proposed trial was ruled incompetent. The German High Seas Fleet, although interned, had not been surrendered and consequently remained German property. A German admiral could not be tried by Britain for destroying German property over which the British had no legal right or jurisdiction.

In the autumn of 1919, the Allies presented their demands for reparations for the scuttled ships in the form of a Protocol to the Treaty of Versailles. Five German light cruisers were to be surrendered within 60 days and 400,000 tons of dock equipment within 90 days. The *B 98*, a German resupply vessel that had arrived at Scapa Flow after the fleet had been scuttled, was to be retained; and the crews of the scuttled ships now held in POW camps would be repatriated on fulfillment of the first two demands.

It was a further seven months before Germany finally signed the Protocol on reparations on 10 January 1920. On 29 January, Von Reuter and the remaining POWs were then taken by train to Hull, where the German steamer *Lisboa* took them home across the North Sea to Wilhelmshaven. They were the last German POWs of World War I to be repatriated – 14 months after the rest of the combatants laid down their arms on Armistice Day, 11 November 1918.

A flotilla of German destroyers came out to greet the *Lisboa* as it approached home waters, and escorted it back to an emotional welcome home. At the quayside, a band played military music as groups of soldiers, sailors, veterans and civilians cheered.

The German sailors who had been shot that fateful day, 21 June 1919, were the last casualties of World War I, which officially ended on 28 June 1919 – only seven days after the might of the German Fleet had sunk dramatically to the bottom of Scapa Flow.

SALVAGING THE FLEET

The British Admiralty's initial reaction to the scuttling of the fleet in 1919 was that the German warships would be left to rot on the bottom of Scapa Flow where they lay. There was to be no question of salvaging them. Naval salvage experts concluded that the wrecks would not prove to be any danger to shipping - but they were soon proved wrong as almost immediately, local vessels started snagging and going aground on the submerged hulls.

The huge war effort had created a vast abundance of ferrous and non-ferrous scrap metal in the form of armaments, shell-casings and the like, which now had no useful purpose; so at first, economically, there was no profit to be made in raising the huge German vessels from their watery tomb. By 1922 however, the market for scrap metal had started to pick up and those with an eye for a profit started to consider raising the sunken leviathans. One of the smaller destroyers, lying in shallower water, was successfully brought to the surface and taken to Stromness for breaking up. On seeing this, the Admiralty changed its policy and invited tenders for salvaging some of the ships. The scuttled destroyers were sold off for £250 each - the far larger battleships were later sold off for £1,000 each. In the following decades, 45 of the 52 warships successfully sent to the bottom were raised to the surface in the greatest marine salvage operation in history – one that continued until 1946.

In 1924, the scrap metal firm of Cox and Danks Ltd, who had started ship-breaking in 1921, bought the massive battlecruisers *Seydlitz* and *Hindenburg* from the Admiralty. They then went on to buy the rest of the fleet – earning the director, Ernest Cox, the title of 'The Man Who Bought a Navy'. When Cox made his decision to lift the fleet, he had never salvaged anything before. He was simply an enterprising scrap metal merchant filled with enthusiasm but with no engineering qualifications. Cox went to Scapa Flow and worked out what had to be done, ignoring the 'experts' who told him it was impossible.

His first salvage attempt was the torpedo-boat destroyer *V 70*, a 924-ton vessel that lay on an even keel in about 15 metres of water. A floating dock was cut into two L-shaped sections that were maneuvered into position on either side of *V 70*. A lifting chain was then passed under her stern from one L-shaped dock section to the other. The chain was tightened at low tide and as the tide subsequently turned and the water level started to rise, the docks and chain strung between them lifted the stern of *V 70* off the bottom. Divers then passed a second chain further along under the keel and this was again tightened at low water. When the tide came in again, the stern of *V 70* was lifted further off the bottom. This process was repeated until there were eventually ten chains in position beneath *V 70*, forming a cradle from end to end.

Just before the tide was about to turn on a cold bright morning in March 1924, Cox gave the signal for his 24 gangs of four winch-men a piece to make six turns on their winches. As the men wound the chain in, the two docks began to tilt noticeably. Another six turns of the winches was ordered

The massive battlecruiser Hindenburg *sits on the bottom after the scuttling. C. W. Burrows*

The battlecruiser Hindenburg *rises from the depths. Courtesy of Orkney Library. William Hourston Collection*

Bringing out the souvenirs. Courtesy Orkney Library. William Hourston Collection

and the 96 winch-men put their backs into it. After yet another six turns, the men felt *V 70* start to lift. Suddenly there was an explosive bang from far below the surface and No. 10 chain whiplashed out of the water. Cox knew that the failure of one chain would fatally overload the nine remaining chains, so he immediately ordered his winch-men to drop everything and hit the deck. As they did so, the other nine chains began to break in quick succession, their half-hundredweight links whipping through the air. Some of the links broke free and hurtled over the heads of the terrified winch-men. Cox himself narrowly missed a serious injury, as a purchase-block gyrated past him, its flailing end almost taking his head off. Mercifully, no one was injured.

From then on, Cox used 12 nine-inch 250-ton wire cables and these proved more reliable than chains. At low water, the wires were wound in tight, and as the tide rose, the ship lifted off the bottom. The pontoons and suspended destroyer were then moved into shallower water until she grounded again. At low water the wires were again wound in and as the tide rose the ship lifted off the bottom and could be moved shallower until she grounded again. Eventually, six weeks later on 4 August 1924 after five such tidal lifts, Cox was able to beach *V 70*. Eleven days after *V 70* was raised, Cox raised the 919-ton torpedo-boat destroyer *S 53*, and in the space of a few months he quickly followed that with *S 55*; and then *G 91*, *G 38* and *S 52*.

In his first year, Cox raised 18 ships, averaging 750 tons each, and by the summer of 1925 he had recovered half of his initial capital outlay of £45,000. Buoyed with success, Cox then purchased a larger floating dock, with which he intended to lift the larger destroyers that were too heavy for the previous pontoons. With this dock he raised all of the remaining destroyers, with the last, the 1,116-ton *G 104*, being raised on 1 May 1926.

In 1926 however a General Strike in Britain caused the price of coal to soar to over £2 per ton. Financially, this was a ruinous price for Cox – one that would close him down in just a few weeks. However, Cox remembered that a diver had reported that the coalbunkers of the huge battlecruiser *Seydlitz* were full. He sent teams of divers down to the wreck and had them cut away the armour plating above her bunkers. Once the bunkers were exposed he had the coal lifted out by mechanical grabs. Cox now had his own private coal supply and his boilers never went cold during the strike, which crippled the rest of the country.

In 1926, he began work on the largest ship in the entire scuttled fleet: the massive 689-foot long, 26,180-ton battlecruiser *Hindenburg*, which sat on the bottom on an even keel in about 21 metres of water. Her distinctive tripod mast and twin funnels still stood proud of the water. She had lain untouched since the day she went down and with a beam of 96 ft and eight 12-inch guns set in four massive turrets (each weighing over 700 tons), she was a huge challenge. Cox decided to pump her dry where she lay and sent divers down to start the laborious task of patching all the 800 openings in her hull by applying instant cement plugs.

After five months of this painstaking work, the hull was nearly water-tight, but it was then discovered that the sealing patches were beginning to fail, letting water in. The local fish, saith, had found that the tallow used on the patches was very palatable and had been eating away at it. The failing patches were refitted with a less tasty mixture which had quick-setting cement in it, and the ship was pumped dry.

When the first attempts were made to lift her, she was found to list severely to one side. She would have capsized, had she not been allowed to sink back down on to the bottom again. Cox had one of the smaller destroyers that had been raised previously grappled to the side of the *Hindenburg* to counter the list. From this grappled destroyer he had a cable run to another salvaged destroyer, which had been beached on the island of Cava about three-quarters of a mile away – using it as a deadweight anchorage for the cable.

On 2 September 1926, *Hindenburg* was successfully raised from the seabed, but shortly afterwards she flooded and sank in a storm. After so many setbacks Cox gave up and abandoned her for the time being. He now focused his salvage efforts on the *Moltke*: another battlecruiser of 22,640 tons, sitting in 24 metres of water. She was a challenge because she lay upside down and at an angle. Her water-line length was just over 610 ft

and she had a beam of 96.5 ft. She had ten 11-inch guns, set in pairs in five turrets, of which three were on the centre-line of the vessel.

Pumps were sent down to the hull and connections for air pipes made along the hull. The pumps were then run day and night and the hull filled with compressed air. With the whole hull a common space, one end of the ship lifted off the seabed with an alarming list and Cox allowed the ship to settle again on the seabed.

Undeterred, Cox then decided to section the hull off into three sealed, airtight compartments to prevent migration of air through the hull and control buoyancy. Compressed air was fed into one section of the hull to create an air bubble, which divers could enter. Every hole in the compartment through which air could escape, then had to be sealed – an extremely time-consuming task made even more difficult by the ship being upside down. Floors and doors were far above their heads and staircases ran the wrong way. The divers had to erect scaffolding to get access to the connecting doors above them.

Cox had a special type of airlock constructed from a line of old boilers, each 6 feet wide by 12 feet high, that he had welded together to form a huge pipe. A number of these pipes were then attached by divers vertically to the upturned whaleback bottom of the hull – reaching all the way up to the surface to form a connecting passageway from the surface to the hull. On the surface, workers climbed into the top of the tube via a hatch and entered a small chamber - which was then pressurised. Once the pressure in the chamber and the rest of the tube had been equalised, another hatch could be opened at the bottom of the chamber. Workers could then climb down a ladder inside the pipe to the hull of the ship far below and, after cutting a manhole into the hull with an oxy-acetylene burner, enter the hull.

Twenty, nine-inch wire lifting-cables were also threaded under the hull and together the combination of compressed air and lifting-cables successfully lifted the ship, upside down, off the bottom to the surface.

On 18 May 1927, the *Moltke* – still upside down – was taken in tow by three tugs down the east coast of Scotland. Her destination was the breakers yard at Rosyth in the Firth of Forth; a journey of about 275 miles.

As the *Moltke* entered the Firth of Forth, disaster nearly struck. The tugs belonged to a German company that Cox had contracted to tow the hull south. Cox had already arranged for an Admiralty pilot to board the lead tug in the Firth of Forth, to guide the hull in its final approach up the Firth to Rosyth. Unfortunately, he had neglected to tell the German contractors of this, and they, in the normal way, had engaged a civilian pilot to do just the same lucrative job. The two pilots came face to face on the tug and a bitter argument developed as to who had the right to guide the *Moltke* in. Both wanted to do it – and neither was prepared to give way to the other. The argument went in circles and as they debated, it escaped their notice that on the incoming tide, the *Moltke* had actually started to make up ground on the tugs. As the *Moltke* gathered momentum, the tow-lines went slack and the pilots suddenly realised that whilst the lead tug was sailing past one side of the rocky islet in the middle of the Forth known as Inchcolm, the accelerating hulk of the *Moltke* was going past the other side. To avert certain disaster, the crew cut away the towing-cables as they began to catch on the rocks. However, directly in the path of the drifting 22,640 tons of German steel and armour plating was that great symbol of Victorian Scotland, the Forth Railway Bridge. The two pilots and tug crews looked on helplessly as the *Moltke* drifted freely and completely out of control towards the great iron structure. A historic catastrophe seemed imminent – but to the relief of the onlookers and the two pilots, the *Moltke* – only by chance – passed harmlessly through the gap between two immense legs of the bridge. She was taken in tow again and led to Rosyth, where she was subsequently broken up.

In 1928, Cox turned his attention to the 24,610-ton battlecruiser *Seydlitz*, which lay in 21 metres of water on her side. After a number of failed lifting attempts she too was eventually brought to the surface. Next, on 30 March 1929, after many long months of painstaking work and from a depth of more than 40 metres, the 24,380-ton battleship *Kaiser* rose off the bottom, tight-sealed and with full buoyancy.

In May 1929, Cox turned his efforts to raising the fast 4,400-ton mine-laying cruiser *Bremse*, which lay capsized on the seabed with a heavy list. Cox had her sealed off into watertight compartments where she lay and she was brought to the surface over a period of two days and taken to Lyness for breaking.

In 1930, Cox decided to have another attempt to lift the 26,180-ton battlecruiser *Hindenburg* – if he could do it, she would be the largest ship ever salvaged. Divers surveyed the ship and reported that some 500 of the original 800 patches were intact. The others had to be repaired or renewed by teams of divers working round the clock. The experience Cox had gained since his earlier attempts to lift her now stood him in good stead. Once pumping was under way, she lifted slowly and evenly off the seabed.

Next on the agenda was the 19,400-ton battlecruiser *Von der Tann*, which lay capsized with a 17½° list, with a water depth over her of 7 to 12 metres. She was sectioned off and made watertight – but during the sealing-off process three workers inside the hull had a narrow escape as they cut through some pipework with oxy-acetylene cutters. The flame ignited a pocket of trapped gas and there was a large explosion, which blew out all the lights and badly damaged the compartment they were working in. All three were injured and water started rushing in. In the darkness, they discovered to their horror that the way out of the cabin was now blocked by a blown-out section of steel bulkhead.

With water continuing to pour into the room, the three men clambered up to the highest point in the cabin, trying to keep their heads above the relentlessly rising water. The water rose as far as their chins, and then miraculously, the sound of rushing water stopped. An air bubble had been formed, and for the time being the immediate prospect of death receded. The cabin was silent, but the men knew that they were on borrowed time and that they would soon use up the precious air.

As soon as the explosion occurred, other men working in the hull in the deck level above, made their way towards the area where the three had been working. From the rooms above, they found that all the surrounding cabins below had filled with seawater – their first thoughts were that the cabin in which the three had been working must be flooded too. They couldn't hear the trapped men's frantic cries for help through the thick armoured deck – even though the trapped men could hear their rescuers above, tapping with hammers on the deck in the hope of getting a response. The trapped men had nothing with which they could signal their presence in return.

As the rescuers waited for a diver to arrive to go down into the flooded deck, one man saw a hose, which led from the cabin below, move. He knew at once that the men were alive and trying to signal their presence. The rescuers then took an all-or-nothing gamble with their own lives to free them, knowing that the trapped men would not have much air left in the flooded cabin. Risking another gas explosion, they used an oxy-acetylene cutter and started cutting through the steel deck to the cabin below. Once the cutting had started, the trapped air bubble was able to filter out through the cut and the water level in the cabin below began to rise again. But, one by one, the rescuers were able to grab hold of the outstretched hands and pluck the trapped men to safety.

In 1933, the last ships Cox would raise – the 19,400-ton battlecruiser *Von der Tann* and the 24,380-ton battleship *Prinzregent Luitpold* – were lifted and towed to Rosyth for breaking. At the end of his eight years of salvage work at Scapa Flow, Cox was £10,000 down.

The Alloa Shipbreaking Co. (later known as Metal Industries) now took over the job of salvaging the remnants of the High Seas Fleet and did so more successfully than Cox. They were able to generate a profit of about £50,000 on each of the larger ships they raised. In June 1933, the 28,075-ton battleship *Bayern* was spectacularly raised from the seabed by compressed air.

The lifts were now becoming more practised and the battleship *Grosser Kurfürst* soon surfaced, followed by the *Kaiserin* in May 1936 and the *Friedrich der Grosse* in April 1937. In 1939, the last of the battlecruisers – the 26,180-ton *Derfflinger* – was raised from the record depth of 45 metres. She was taken to Rosyth for breaking but the outbreak of war halted her being scrapped. She remained afloat, awaiting her final fate throughout World War II, until finally being taken apart in 1946. She was the last of the High Seas Fleet to be salvaged whole.

From 1962 onwards, smaller-scale salvage works were carried out on the sunken battleships *König*, *Kronprinz Wilhelm* and *Markgraf*, with holes being blasted into the hulls around the engine and boiler room areas as well as the magazines and torpedo-tube areas of the hulls. The blasting opened up the hulls and allowed access for salvage divers to get in and free up non-ferrous fitments in preparation for lifting them to the surface. Similar works were carried out on the light cruisers. All the remaining wrecks bear the scars of this salvage work.

The steel of the German wrecks was forged before or during WWI – before the first nuclear bomb at Hiroshima in 1945 – and so has lower levels of radiation than modern steel. Some steel plating was removed from several of the wrecks for the manufacture of sensitive medical instruments.

The last salvage works were carried out in the late 1970s and the wrecks in recent years have been scheduled as historic monuments, to make sure they are preserved for the future.

THE BATTLESHIPS TODAY

SMS *König* (Battleship – *König class*)

Seiner Majestät Schiff (SMS) *König* was one of the eleven battleships in the interned German High Seas Fleet. Of those eleven, three remain on the bottom of Scapa Flow today: *König*, *Kronprinz Wilhelm* and *Markgraf*. They sit in depths ranging from 38 metres to 45 metres, with their shallowest areas rising to just 15-20 metres from the surface – easily in reach for today's sport divers.

SMS *König* was built by Kaiserliches Werft in Wilhelmshaven on Germany's small piece of western coastline that fronts the North Sea. She gave her name to the fourth class (König class) of German dreadnoughts, the successors to the preceding Kaiser class. The Kaiser class battleships had five twin 12-inch gun-turrets as their primary armament, set one on the foredeck towards the bow, two aft at the stern and one either side of the

The German battleship SMS König.

world had ever seen – so much bigger than their predecessors that the Kiel Canal had to be specially widened to let them through after their completion. She was designed to displace 25,796 tons, but at combat load with her magazines full she displaced 28,600-tons. Even so, powered by three coal/oil-fired turbines, her three great propellers could still drive her up to 23 knots. At a cruising speed of 12 knots, she had a design range of 8,000 nautical miles.

König was 575 ft long – the length of two football pitches – with a beam of 97 ft and a draft of over 30 ft. Her main armour belt, which ran along the waterline of her hull on either side, was 13.8 inches thick. Her deck had a 3.8-inch layer of armour plating on it as protection against falling shot. Her main armament was ten 12-inch guns

ship midships in a staggered 'wing' arrangement. For the König class, one of the wing turrets was moved forward and placed in a superfiring position on the foredeck – sitting behind and above the most forward turret. The other wing turret was moved to the centre-line of the vessel amidships. This new arrangement meant that in a broadside salvo, all ten 12-inch guns could be fired simultaneously – as opposed to just eight in the Kaiser class battleships.

König was launched on 1 March 1913 and commissioned into the German Imperial Navy on 10 August 1914. *König* and her sister dreadnoughts *Kronprinz* and *Markgraf* were some of the largest dreadnoughts that the

set in five twin turrets, each with 11.8-inch thick side armour plating and weighing more than 600-tons. These massive guns could hurl shells, each one capable of destroying a lesser ship, some 22,300 yards – more than twelve miles. The Gun Room of each turret was connected to a revolving ammunition hoist and Transfer Room, which led down inside an armoured barbette to the magazine below it at the bottom of the ship.

Along each side of her hull above the armour belt were set seven 5.9-inch rapid-fire casemate guns, each on its own rotating pedestal and protected by a 6.75-inch thick armoured turret-front that rotated with the gun. These secondary armament casemate guns were designed to protect the battleship

© Rod Macdonald

The wreck of the battleship König.

against smaller ships such as torpedo-boat destroyers trying to close for a broadside torpedo shot. Each 5.9-inch casemate gun could hurl seven 101-lb shells per minute over a distance of eight miles.

By the time of her scuttling, her original eight smaller 3.45-inch quick firing casemate guns had been replaced with four 3.45-inch anti-aircraft guns to counter the new threat from the air. As was customary for dreadnought era battleships she was fitted with five 20-inch submerged torpedo tubes – one at the bow and four in the beam set two on either side of the ship. She was thus heavily protected as well as being fitted with a ferocious array of firepower. At this time, battleships were considered almost indestructible. She carried a complement of 1,136 officers and men.

König was the flagship of V Division of III Battle Squadron (of three Squadrons) of the German High Seas Fleet at the famous Battle of Jutland that took place in the North Sea in May 1916 (called the 'Battle of Skagerrak' by the Germans). She was the lead battleship of the fleet's vanguard and under her command were her three sister ships, *Markgraf, Kronprinz Wilhelm* and *Grosser Kurfürst*.

The Battle of Jutland was the first major naval encounter between the British Grand Fleet and the German High Seas Fleet and was the greatest clash of steel warships the world had seen. Although numerically, at the end of the day the British came off worse in numbers of ships sunk and men killed, the Germans had a higher number of ships badly damaged and tactically were outplayed when the main element of the British Grand Fleet joined the battle after arriving from Scapa Flow. The Royal Navy was able to maintain its naval blockade of Germany in the English Channel and the North Sea – and this was instrumental in starving the German people and her military, weakening morale and leading to Germany's eventual submission.

The initial bloody skirmishes of the Battle were between the High Seas Fleet and the British Battlecruiser Fleet – which was out scouting under the command of Admiral Sir David Beatty. The opening encounter saw the complete destruction of the British battlecruisers HMS *Indefatigable* and HMS *Queen Mary* in catastrophic magazine explosions. However, when the main British Grand Fleet from Scapa Flow entered the fray, the Germans were well and truly on the run for the remainder of the battle. Admiral Sir John Jellicoe, in very difficult conditions and with limited and poor information from his commanders, skillfully controlled the battle and outmanoeuvred the German Fleet as it tried to run for the safety of its home base.

Unbeknown to the Germans, the British had some time previously broken German naval codes. Intelligence was received suggesting that the entire German High Seas Fleet had put to sea to harass British shipping and that they were expecting only to meet elements of the British Battlecruiser Fleet. The 52 warships of the Battlecruiser Fleet, under the command of Admiral Sir David Beatty, were tasked out of the Firth of Forth to patrol in the North Sea and search for the German Fleet. Battlecruisers had the same powerful guns as battleships, but being designed for greater speed carried far less protective armour against plunging fire than battleships. Their vulnerabilities were not fully appreciated at the time – but would be tragically exposed during the Battle.

On 31 May, the British Battlecruiser Fleet unknowingly entered an area in close proximity to the full German High Seas Fleet – the two sides were about 20 miles apart but completely unaware of the other's presence. A neutral Danish steamship by chance steamed in between the two fleets and was spotted simultaneously by both sides, although the respective fleets could still not see one another. Light cruisers were sent out by both sides to investigate the steamship – and as they closed, they each caught sight of the other's cruisers. As soon as reports of the encounter came back, Beatty attacked with the main battlecruiser group. The German scouting light cruisers turned and fled towards the safety of their own main fleet, pursued by Beatty – who at first thought it was a German battlecruiser group he had encountered.

Battle commenced at about 2.20 p.m. and raged throughout the afternoon as the two lines of warships, each about eight miles long, wheeled and tried to outmanoeuvre each other. *König, Markgraf* and the battlecruisers *Lützow* and *Derfflinger* took ten direct hits from 40 salvoes fired by the British battle group in one skirmish. At 4.05 p.m., a series of salvoes from the 18,700-ton battlecruiser *Von Der Tann* struck the last ship of the British line: the battlecruiser HMS *Indefatigable*. She blew up in a cataclysmic magazine explosion, in which 1,015 men died instantly. Only three of her crew survived.

The 26,000-ton battle cruiser HMS *Queen Mary* was targeted by the mighty guns of *Derfflinger* and *Seydlitz* and in a hail of fire she also exploded and sank quickly with the loss of 1,274 crew. There were only eight survivors.

The British cruiser *Southampton* was sent to scout some way ahead of the battle and reported to Beatty that it was not simply a force of German battlecruisers that had been encountered – it was the full German High Seas Fleet, packed full of almost indestructible battleships, all steaming at full speed towards the action.

In the face of the over whelming firepower of the entire German High Seas Fleet, Beatty wheeled his ships to the south to let the Germans catch full sight of them and then altered course to run northwards in front of the German Fleet – who thought they had gained the opportunity of annihilating the entire British Battlecruiser Fleet. However, Beatty was luring the German Fleet into the jaws of the 72 ships of the British Grand Fleet, which, on receiving intelligence reports of the planned German sortie, had put to sea from Scapa Flow before the German Fleet had even left port – and was charging down from the north at full speed to a pre-arranged rendezvous point with the Battlecruiser Fleet.

Beatty's calculated manoeuvre took the British rearguard ships *Malaya* and *Warspite* within range of the big guns of the German vanguard battleships – at the forefront of which was *König*. The British ships could make 24 knots whilst the German battleships could only make 23 knots. Eventually this small difference in top speed took their vessels outwith the range of the German guns and then from a safe distance, the British guns (which had a superior range) kept up a murderous hail of fire on the German lead ships as Beatty led them into the trap.

Admiral Sir John Jellicoe, in command of the arriving British Grand Fleet, then managed to accomplish the classic naval manoeuvre of 'crossing the T'. The whole Grand Fleet lined up (unseen at first) in the path of the onrushing German column of battleships and then appearing from beneath the horizon, crossed in line astern, directly in the path of the German battle line. Every British warship could simultaneously fire broadsides at the German line, but only the lead German vessels could return fire with their forward big guns. The German vanguard was faced with a complete line of British dreadnoughts belching fire at them – which stretched along the horizon to the north-east and north-west for as far as the eye could see. Salvo following salvo rained down on the German vanguard. *König* – the lead dreadnought of the vanguard – was badly hit many times and soon took on a 4½° list. The *Lützow* – the flagship of the German battlecruiser squadron – was hit many times and withdrew and sank shortly afterwards.

Realizing that a trap had been sprung, the Germans tried to escape from the cauldron of death and the whole fleet turned to flee to the south. *Derfflinger* sighted the British battlecruiser HMS *Invincible* silhouetted on the northern horizon 10,000 yards away and commenced firing at her. *Invincible* was struck and broke in two before sinking with huge loss of life.

Admiral Scheer then turned his fleet to the east as British guns continued to pound his ships remorselessly. Some German ships turned away without waiting for orders, causing others to take evasive action. *König* was turned into the wind and created a smokescreen to cover the German withdrawal, as simultaneously, German torpedo-boats made a fast attack on the British battleships. The combination of smokescreen and torpedo attack caused the British to take evasive action and in the confusion of the German counter-attack, the main German Fleet was able to disappear from sight in the fading light.

Jellicoe formed his fleet up into night cruising stations and positioned his fleet across the route that the Germans would want to take if they attempted to flee back to their naval base. He hoped to block the German

Shipwreck – the essentials

Type of wreck	König class battleship
Nationality	German
Year of construction	1914
Dimensions	575 ft x 97 ft x 30 ft
Displacement (tons)	25,390 – design; 28,600 – full load
Date sunk	21 June 1919
Cause of sinking	scuttled
Depth of water	42 metres
Least depth above wreck	20 metres
Position	58 53.220N, 003 09.002W

any further fleet action against the British. Whatever numerical success the German Navy could claim, the Royal Navy was able to maintain its blockade of German ports and continue starving both the civilian population and the troops on the Western Front into submission. The High Seas Fleet had not so much gained a victory as it had escaped annihilation once the full might of Jellicoe's Grand Fleet had arrived from Scapa Flow.

The vast majority of the damage to British ships was suffered by Beatty's Battlecruiser Fleet – and the attached 5th Battle Squadron of four dreadnought battleships. The Grand Fleet was able to report itself ready for sea again on the evening of 2 June, with 22 of its 24 capital ships serviceable. In fact, the return of the dreadnought battleships HMS *Queen Elizabeth* and HMS *Emperor of India* from refit and the completion of the three last Revenge class battleships gave the Grand Fleet back its full might.

The High Seas Fleet however, badly battered and bruised, limped back to its base at Wilhelmshaven. Of the 16 German capital ships that fought, only eight were fit for action after the battle. Of the five German battlecruisers involved in the battle, only two were fit for action some two months later.

König continued to serve in the fleet and was involved in the conquest of the Baltic Islands in the autumn of 1917. She turned turtle and sank to the bottom of Scapa Flow at 2 p.m. on the day of the scuttle, 21 June 1919.

Today *König* lies in 42 metres of water east of the island of Cava at Lat. 58° 53.220N, 003° 09.002W. When she was scuttled the thousands of gallons of seawater that poured into her altered her buoyancy and she became unstable. The colossal weight of her superstructure and her five main gun-turrets, each weighing more than 700 tons, caused her to list and then turn turtle. She now lies almost completely upside down with her starboard side main deck only a few feet above the bottom. Her superstructure is deeply embedded in the fine silty seabed, with most of it being below the level of the seabed. The least depth down to her hull is about 20 metres.

König has been extensively salvaged over the years and much has been

retreat home as he waited for dawn – when he hoped to sight and annihilate the German Fleet. Skirmishing between elements of the two fleets continued after darkness had fallen.

The last shots were fired at about 3.20 a.m. as Scheer boldly managed to take his fleet directly through the lighter destroyers and cruisers at the rear of the British line and escape back to base. The battle had lasted for 11 hours, during which time the German High Seas Fleet had lost one pre-dreadnought battleship, one battlecruiser, four cruisers and five destroyers, with 2,551 German sailors killed and 507 wounded. The British Grand Fleet came off numerically worse with the loss of three battlecruisers, three cruisers and eight destroyers. A total of 6,094 British servicemen were killed in action, 674 were wounded. The Germans took prisoner 177 British servicemen. The statistics do not however take account of the much higher ratio of damaged ships on the German side, or the fact that once the main British Grand Fleet engaged, the German Fleet was on the back foot for the remainder of the battle. The Royal Navy retained undisputed mastery of the seas and as a result, the German High Seas Fleet was deterred from

The wreck of the battleship Kronprinz Wilhelm *with, in the background, her sister dreadnoughts* Markgraf *and* König.

© Rod Macdonald

removed from her. In the 1970s, Scapa Flow Salvage Co. blew off the 25-ton plates of her side armour belt - and also removed the thick armoured bulkhead of the citadel that ran across the ship from side in front of the foremost main armament 12-inch gun turret. The citadel was essentially an armoured box inside which all the important parts of the ship were protected. This blasting has led to the collapse of the structure of the bow section.

Nundy (Marine Metals) Ltd blasted open the hull in the vicinity of the engine and boiler rooms as well as the magazines and torpedo rooms, to allow salvage divers to remove the valuable non-ferrous metal fitments there.

Along the port side of the wreck, the removal of the armour belt has left the vertical structural beams, which are spaced every six feet or so, standing exposed. Divers can pass through these to enter the large space between the beams and the inner square box of the ship and pass almost the full length of the hull inside. On the upturned flat bottom of the hull, the salvage damage is everywhere with much hull plating being removed. One of the two rudders still stands in place – the other has been knocked from its mount. The aft athwartships section of citadel that protected the aftmost 12-inch gun-turret barbette is still in place, curving round the barbette. Behind it, the barbette of the superimposed 12-inch gun-turret can be made out amidst the wreckage.

Although the bottom of the hull has largely been removed around the engine rooms, towards the bow and near the stern, sections remain intact. Here, stretches of her docking keels, steel boxes running the length of the hull and filled with oiled wood, are still visible. Large bilge keels – thin strips of steel 3–4 ft high – run along either side of the hull bottom, designed to give its flat shape a cutting edge for manoeuvering.

SMS *Kronprinz Wilhelm* (**Battleship** – *König class*)

Seiner Majestät Schiff (SMS) *Kronprinz* was built by Germaniawerft, in Kiel, as part of the arms race, which started in the 1890s, intended to allow the German Imperial Navy to challenge the traditional supremacy of the Royal Navy. She was launched on 21 February 1914 and commissioned into the German Imperial Navy on 8 November 1914. Her name was latterly changed to *Kronprinz Wilhelm* on 27 January 1918, in honour of Kaiser Wilhelm II on his 59th birthday.

Kronprinz was a König class battleship – the same class and specifications as her sister dreadnought *König* (which had given her name to the class of four such ships – the other two of the class being *Markgraf* and *Grosser Kurfürst*).

The *Kronprinz* was 575 ft long – the length of two football pitches – and had a beam of 97 ft and a draft of over 30 ft. She displaced 25,388 tons, but fully loaded for combat she displaced 28,600 tons. Battleships protected their most important and vulnerable parts inside an armoured box called

Above left: Double bottom framing on Kronprinz Wilhelm © *Ewan Rowell*

Above: The German battleship Kronprinz Wilhelm.

the 'citadel', which ran from just in front of the forward gun-turrets all the way back to aft of the stern gun-turrets. Along the side of the citadel on either side of the ship at the waterline ran the main armour belt, which was 13.8 inches thick. In front of the forward gun-turrets and aft of the stern gun-turrets, the armour belt crossed the ship from one side of the hull to the other, where it joined up with the other side armour belt.

When the first generations of pre-dreadnoughts and dreadnoughts were developed, the less powerful guns of the day fired in a relatively flat trajectory – which meant that the shells fired were more likely to hit the side armour belt of the foe – rather than the deck. But as battleships developed, the size of their guns and the range of those guns increased. More powerful guns could fire from far greater distances and this increased the height of a shell's trajectory producing 'plunging fire' or 'falling shot' – which became more likely to strike the more lightly armoured deck than the thick side armour belt. As protection against plunging fire, *Kronprinz*'s deck had a 3.8-inch layer of armour plating.

Her main armament was ten 12-inch guns, set in five twin-turrets, each with 11.8-inch thick side armour plating and weighing more than 700-tons. Two super-firing turrets were set one behind the other towards the bow - in front of the conning tower and superstructure. Another was set midships and the remaining two set towards the stern, one behind the other. These massive guns could hurl shells some 21,000 yards.

Along each side of her hull above the main armour belt were seven secondary armament 5.9-inch rapid-fire casemate guns, each set in its own rotating pedestal and protected by a 6.75-inch thick armoured turret-front, which rotated with the gun. These casemate guns were designed to protect the battleship against smaller ships, such as torpedo-boat destroyers trying to close for a broadside shot at the battleship. Each 5.9-inch casemate gun could hurl seven 101-lb shells per minute over a distance of eight miles. When she was built she was originally fitted with an additional six smaller 3.45-inch quick firing casemate guns – but in light of the new threat from the skies, these were later removed and she was fitted with four 3.45-inch

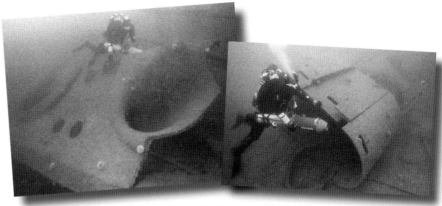

Above left: Anchor hawses on the Kroprinz Wilhelm © *Ewan Rowell*

Above right: A diver hangs beside the spotting top on the battleship Kronprinz Wilhelm © *Ewan Rowell*

anti aircraft guns mounted either side of the rear conning tower. In common with all dreadnoughts of the time, she was fitted with five submerged 20-inch torpedo tubes; one at the bow and four in the beam, two either side.

Her 46,000 horsepower turbines drove three huge propellers that made the *Kronprinz* the fastest in her class, with a top speed of about 23 knots. She carried a crew of 1,136 men.

Kronprinz formed part of the V Division of III Battle Squadron of the High Seas Fleet and fought at the Battle of Jutland, being the fourth in line of seven battleships. Although her sister ships *König* and *Markgraf* were badly damaged in the thick of the battle, *Kronprinz* came through unscathed and kept up a murderous hail of fire on the British battleships without the loss of any of her crew.

Apart from this crucial battle, *Kronprinz* saw action on only one other occasion – an encounter that she almost did not survive. At 10.30 p.m. on 4 November 1916, Admiral Hipper led *Kronprinz* together with *König*, *Markgraf* and *Grosser Kurfürst* out from their base to support a squadron of destroyers going to the rescue of *U-20*, which had run aground off the Danish coast. The scale of the operation was unusual and resulted from the presence of one man marooned in the U-boat: the commander, Kapitänleutnant Walther Schwieger. He had been responsible for one of World War I's most infamous events: the torpedoing of the *Lusitania* off southern Ireland with the loss of 1,198 men, women and children.

The destroyers tried to take *U-20* in tow but she was so well entrenched in the sand that their hawsers snapped. All other efforts to get *U-20* off the sandbank failed and so the following morning her crew were taken off - and she was blown up where she lay. At about 11 a.m. the battle group turned to head for home but at about 11.20 a.m., the group was spotted by the British submarine *J 1*, commanded by Commander Noel Laurence. After closing unseen and taking up a firing position, at 12.08 p.m. he fired his first torpedo, which successfully struck *Grosser Kurfürst*. He then fired a second torpedo that hit *Kronprinz* and blasted a gaping hole in her side. Both stricken battleships started flooding with tons of water and it was only their watertight compartments that prevented them from sinking and allowed them to limp back to the safe haven of their base. Both battleships had been put out of action for several months as a result of Commander Laurence's daring piece of seamanship - and in recognition of his actions, and for surviving two hours of depth charging by the German destroyers, he was awarded a bar to his Distinguished Service Order. *Kronprinz* spent most of the rest of the war at her moorings.

In the spring of 1918, the Germans had mounted a major offensive in the Somme and in August 1918, the Allies began a counter-offensive using new artillery techniques and methods and drove the Germans out of all the ground they had taken in their Spring Offensive. By September 1918 the Allies had broken through the Hindenburg Line – it was the final nail in the coffin of any German hopes of winning the war.

By October 1918, the British naval blockade was strangling and starving both the German homeland and also her troops on the Western Front. It had become clear that the war was lost and German politicians were compelled to try and negotiate a peaceful end to the war. German naval commanders however planned a last-ditch, all-or-nothing battle,

to try and destroy the British Grand Fleet and thereby secure a better bargaining position for any subsequent peace negotiations.

The plan was for German destroyers to raid Allied shipping off the coast of Flanders and the Thames Estuary – while the main German battle fleet secretly gathered at the Schillig Roadstead anchorage. It was hoped that the destroyer action would attract the British Grand Fleet and lure it towards Terschelling, a Dutch island some 70 miles from the Ems River estuary. In this killing-ground, mines had already been sewn and 25 U-boats lurked at the ready. Once the U-boats and mines had weakened the British Grand Fleet, the massive firepower of the German High Seas Fleet would be brought to bear on to their unsuspecting foe. The British Grand Fleet would be decimated.

The plan, however, was leaked and swept around the German sailors in the fleet like wildfire, getting more and more exaggerated as it went. Soon there were rumours that the German High Seas Fleet had accepted a British challenge for a fight to the death; that the 69-year-old Admiral Von Tirpitz had come out of retirement to take charge of the fleet to lead it to its *Götterdämmerung*; and even that the Kaiser himself would sail with the fleet.

The morale of the crews however was very poor: they all realised that the war was lost and were unwilling to risk their lives on a glorified but meaningless show of force. The crews of the *Kronprinz*, *König* and *Markgraf* refused to obey their orders to leave harbour. The mutiny spread and the plan was postponed as time after time the men refused to action their orders to put to sea. In frustration, on 31 October, the German Command had *U-135* stand off the *Thüringen*, which was in open mutiny, and 200 marines were put aboard. The mutineers fled to the fo'c'stle and stood firm there. Other mutineers on the nearby *Helgoland* trained its guns on *U-135* and its accompanying destroyers. As the crisis escalated, the mutineers on the *Helgoland* found to their astonishment that the guns of the *Thüringen*, now in the hands of loyal troops, were being trained on them. The standoff lasted for some time until the mutineers gave way. Some 500 men from the *Thüringen* and *Helgoland* were arrested.

The Third Squadron with the *Kronprinz*, *König* and *Markgraf* was sent to Kiel as the fleet was dispersed. There, mutiny flared again and this time as the rebellion grew, it won the support of the townspeople. On 4 November, the mutineers won control of Kiel. The rebellion then spread from town to town, with communist red flags appearing everywhere. On 9 November, the Kaiser abdicated and gave way to a communist regime.

At 5 a.m., on Monday, 11 November 1918, the Armistice, suspending the hostilities, was signed. By the time she was scuttled in June 1919, the *Kronprinz* had only a skeleton crew of only about 20 men, and her guns had been disarmed before she had set off from Germany for internment in Scapa Flow. She finally slipped beneath the waves to her present resting place at 1.15 p.m. on the day of the scuttling.

Today, the *Kronprinz Wilhelm* lies upside down in about 38 metres of water at 58° 53.669N, 003° 09.823W. She rests on her starboard main deck with much of her superstructure embedded in the silty bottom. The drop down from the surface to the highest point of the wreck – her flat keel – is only 12 to 15 metres.

Salvers removed her 13.8-inch thick armour belt along each side of the hull in the 1970s, and at the same time blasted open the hull from one side to the other in front of the forward gun-turrets, and removed the armoured bulkhead of the citadel. This blasting at the bow has caused the ship to lose its strength here – and the whole bow section forward of the 12-inch gun turrets has collapsed. However, the two massive forward gun-turrets with their armoured barbettes, the conning tower, superstructure and midships twin 12-inch gun turret, allied to the two aftmost twin 12-inch turrets and the horizontal armour deck give the midships section of the hull great strength. The hull reforms here at the forward turrets – the upturned whaleback of the hull bottom being a flat expanse almost 100 ft wide and lined for almost the entire length of the ship with rectangular docking keels, long steel boxes filled with oiled wood on which the ship would rest in dry dock. At each side of the hull is a long slender bilge keel some 3–4 ft high, which gave the flat bottom a cutting edge for maneuvering.

Towards the stern there is a fair amount of damage to her hull in the vicinity of the engine rooms, boiler rooms, and torpedo rooms – the result of blasting by salvers to allow divers to get access to the valuable non-ferrous metals in these areas. In particular, there is a large hole about 15 metres across blasted in her port side about two-thirds of the way back towards her stern, which is fringed by torn plating.

Along the topmost edge of the hull and projecting down the side is a latticework of keel framing from the double bottom beams. The whole vertical side armour belt below has been salved and removed to reveal the 1-inch thick internal steel box of the ship's structure.

On the port side, at a depth of 30 metres the square box of the inner ship seems to flare outwards to a flatter section – the casemate deck. Here, the inverted bulwark rail of the ship comes into view, marking the end of the hull. The main deck here now runs in below the ship towards the superstructure, which is well embedded in the silt.

Although the flat bottom of the hull has a noticeable slope from the higher port side downwards, the seemingly delicate rounded stern of the ship lies flat on its quarterdeck, the hull ringed with rows of portholes. High above, both rudders still stand proud, the starboard-side rudder running roughly fore and aft and the portside rudder skewed at an angle.

Her massive propellers were salved aeons ago and the hull has been blown open around the propeller shafts. Moving forward from the stern along the port side, approaching the massive aftmost 12-inch gun-turret, it becomes clear that the whole hull has twisted, having lost its structural integrity as a result of the salvage blasting. Whereas the very stern section of the hull sits flat on the seabed, at the aftmost main 12-inch gun turret, the main deck lifts off the seabed quite dramatically – the metal of the hull curling up and over the 12-inch gun turrets. From being flat on the seabed, the hull here assumes its more angular, port side up aspect. At this dramatic stress-change in the orientation of the wreck, divers can venture under the overhanging main deck into the pitch darkness and locate the aftmost twin 12-inch gun-turret. These are the most accessible of all the remaining big guns that fired at the Battle of Jutland. Both barrels are clear of the seabed, their ends jammed into the teak deck planking above.

Moving further forward from the aftmost turret, divers are confronted with a seemingly flat wall of steel. This is the bottom section of the after superimposed 12-inch gun-turret, which sat higher (and now lower) than the aftmost turret. Consequently, its top is now buried in the seabed and its twin barrels appear to lie on the seabed half covered by silt.

Along the bulwark rail there are rows of portholes – some still in place, countersunk with brass screws. *Kronprinz* had seven 5.9-inch casemate guns along either side of her hull on her battery deck, set on rotating pedestals inside a 6.75-inch-thick steel rotating turret-front. After passing the two main aft 12-inch gun-turrets, the first of two of these casemate guns appears. The aftmost turret barrel points dead astern, while the turret further forward has its barrel pointing outwards directly away from the hull.

Beyond this second casemate gun, the hull loses its shape and is a jumble of torn, bent and buckled plating often with large portholes dotted along the former hull plates. Passing over this salvaged area, the four-feet-wide foremast lies on the seabed at 90° to the hull. It is practically intact and the cross rigging lies nearby. Some way along the mast, the armoured spotting top is still in place, ringed with its viewing slits and inside, still displaying the communications equipment. The seabed along both sides of the great hull is littered with wreckage and rigging.

The armoured box, or the 'citadel', which housed the massively strong gun-turrets, is holding the main central part of the *Kronprinz* together. As with the stern section – which has twisted to sit flat on the seabed, beyond the forward extent of the citadel – towards the bow – the hull loses its structural integrity. The hull seems to stop abruptly as though sliced across, and forward of the citadel the bow section has collapsed to lie almost flat on the seabed, its plates buckled and lying over each other. Portholes still line the jumbled plating, and perhaps the most visually stunning sight is the two massive anchor hawses with two large portholes in between.

Shipwreck – the essentials

Type of wreck	König class battleship
Nationality	German
Year of construction	1914
Dimensions	575 ft x 97 ft x 30 ft
Displacement (tons)	25,390 – design: 28,600 – full load
Date sunk	21 June 1919
Cause of sinking	scuttled
Depth of water	38 metres
Least depth above wreck	12 metres
Position	58 53.669N, 003 09.823W

SMS *Markgraf* (Battleship – *König class*)

The König class battleship *Markgraf* was built in Germany by A. G. Weser at Bremen to the same specifications as her sister dreadnoughts *König* and *Kronprinz*. She was laid down in November 1911, launched on 4 June 1913 and commissioned into the German Imperial Navy on 1 October 1914. *Markgraf* and the other König class battleships – *König*, *Kronprinz* and *Grosser Kurfürst* – were the most modern, most heavily armoured and gunned ships of the German Fleet and so were assigned as the vanguard, the 5th Division (V) of III Battle Squadron of the High Seas Fleet. They were the first of three battleship units. Following directly astern were the older Kaiser class battleships of VI Division, III Battle Squadron; then the Helgoland and Nassau class ships of I Battle Squadron; and then in the rear guard were the elderly Deutschland class pre-dreadnoughts of II Battle Squadron.

Being in the heart of the vanguard, *Markgraf* was at the front of the action and took part in some of the heavier fighting in the Battle of Jutland. She scored hits on the British battlecruiser *Tiger* at a range of 21,000 yards and also on the battlecruiser *Princess Royal*, the cruiser *Warrior* and the

Left: The German battleship Markgraf.

Below: The wreck of the battleship Markgraf.

© Rod Macdonald

armoured cruiser *Defence*. She herself was attacked with torpedoes on several occasions by British destroyers and received five large calibre British 15-inch shell hits, losing 23 of her crew. *Markgraf* subsequently took part in Operation Albion, the conquest of the Russian-held Baltic Islands of the Gulf of Riga in 1917.

On 21 June 1919 – the date of the fateful scuttle at Scapa Flow – a Royal Marine boarding party boarded *Markgraf* as she began to settle into the water. The Royal Marines had their orders to stop the battleship sinking and once aboard, confronted *Markgraf*'s captain, Lt-Cdr Walther Schumann, who was busy below helping to complete the final operations to ensure she sank. He eventually emerged from below deck waving a white flag. He refused to obey orders from the Royal Marines to have his own men go below and shut off the flood valves, and refused to allow the Marines to go below to do so. A scuffle broke out in which Schumann was shot through the head. His fleet engineer, Faustmann, managed to stay below and complete the work and *Markgraf* went to the bottom at about 4.45 p.m. Lt-Cdr Schumann's grave can be seen at the Royal Naval Cemetery at Lyness on the island of Hoy, along with the graves of the other German sailors who died that day and many British seamen from both wars.

Today *Markgraf* lies upturned and resting on her portside main deck at 58° 53.505N, 03° 09.928W. The depth to the seabed is about 45 metres and the least depth over her is about 24 metres. She is the most intact of the three German battleships – partly protected by her depth, which made salvage difficult, and partly because Metal Industries carried out only limited salvage works. They had left her unworked so that they could lift her with compressed air in the same manner as had Cox & Danks decades earlier – but they never did.

The port side of her hull rests on the seabed, so on this side you can get no glimpse of the superstructure of the vessel. On the higher starboard side of the hull, as you descend, the hull stops abruptly at the bulwark rail in about 40 metres of water. From here down to the seabed at 45 metres is a several-metre-high chasm. The teak-planked deck runs off sharply under the hull, creating a black, eerie cave under the overhanging deck, which reveals part of the superstructure of the battleship. The midships twin 12-inch gun-turret can be found half-buried in the shale with the starboard crane stanchion just aft of it.

Shipwreck – the essentials	
Type of wreck	König class battleship
Nationality	German
Year of construction	1913
Dimensions	575 ft x 97 ft x 30 ft
Displacement (tons)	25,390 – design: 28,600 – full load
Date sunk	21 June 1919
Cause of sinking	scuttled
Depth of water	45 metres
Least depth above wreck	24 metres
Position	58° 53.505N, 03° 09.928W

The very stem of the bow is intact and drops off majestically straight down from 25–30 metres to the seabed at 45 metres. Moving aft on top of the hull, however, there is much structural damage just beyond the intact stem. Here, a large section of the complete hull has sagged downwards for some 5–10 metres, from a depth of 25 metres to a depth of 35 metres. This collapsed section runs aft for some way until the hull reforms at a mass of jagged and bent plating. This marks the forward bulkhead of the armoured box (the 'citadel') where salvers blasted directly across the hull to get at the valuable armour bulkhead. It is the huge armoured strength of the citadel, with its forward and after gun-turrets and barbettes, conning tower and superstructure, after turrets and horizontal armour deck that has kept the mid section of the hull intact and allowed the more fragile section forward of the citadel to collapse.

Moving aft from here on top of the wreck, the massive 100 foot wide flat expanse of the keel seems like an endless plateau punctured by the outline of plating and rivets, with the occasional round water intake. Two bilge keels – strips of steel some three feet high – line either side of the hull, designed to give the flat bottom of the hull a cutting edge for turning.

A massive anchor-chain runs athwartships, just aft of the blasted area near the bow, and drops away down the starboard side to the seabed. As the ship at anchor turned turtle on the surface during the scuttling, it wrapped its anchor chain around the upturned hull. Portholes line the sides of the hull near the seabed until the hull recedes to form the casemate gun deck where the 5.9-inch rapid-firing casemate guns can be found, set

Above left: A diver illuminates a searchlight. SMS Brummer © *Bob Anderson*

Above: The German light cruiser SMS Brummer.

in their individual armoured turrets and protected by a 6.75-inch-thick steel rotating turret front.

On top of the wreck, towards the stern, in the vicinity of the engine rooms, a large hole some 15 metres by 15 metres has been blasted into the hull from above by salvers to allow access to the valuable non-ferrous fitments in the engine rooms. The hole drops down through several deck levels.

The majority of her 13.8-inch vertical side armour belt was removed by the salvage work of the 1970s, leaving the latticework of her double bottom-framing visible at the sides. Ragged metal runs along the hull where the armour plate has been blasted off. A few smaller armour plates remain in place towards the bow and the stern.

Aft of the last casemate gun, the main hull reforms, the sides hard down in the sand and sweeping back towards the seemingly fragile and delicate stern, again lined by portholes. Atop the keel, both her massive angular rudders still stand proud. All of her three propellers have been removed and just forward of the rudders, ugly scars and torn plating reveal where the free sections of shaft entered the hull.

THE LIGHT CRUISER WRECKS TODAY

SMS *Brummer* (Light cruiser, Bremse class)

The *Kleiner Kreuzer, Seiner Majestät Minendampfer* (SMS) *Brummer* was a fast mine-laying light cruiser, built at Stettin by A. G. Vulcan. Launched on 11 December 1915, she was completed and commissioned into the German High Seas Fleet on 2 April 1916 – although she did not take part in the Battle of Jutland with the Fleet a month later. Her design displacement was 4,308 tons but fully laden for combat she would displace 5,856 tons. Driven by her two sets of steam turbines and twin propellers, she could achieve speeds of up to 28 knots – far faster than the battleships of the time, which could make 23 knots. Her name, *Brummer*, means 'bluebottle' in German.

The wreck of the light cruiser SMS Brummer at Scapa Flow with, inset, the wreck as it looked in 1989. Note how the foredeck 5.9-inch gun has fallen from its mount to the seabed.

© Rod Macdonald

Brummer was 462 ft in length with a beam of 44 ft and a draft of 20 ft. She was built for speed to penetrate enemy seas, lay her deadly cargo of up to 450 mines and outrun any enemy vessel that might try to close on her. To keep her weight down she was lightly protected with 1.6-inch main belt armour plating along her sides. The nerve centre of the ship in battle was the fire control tower, and this was more heavily protected with 3.8-inch armour plating. The armoured deck had 0.6-inch plating as a minimal protection against plunging fire. She carried a crew of 309 officers and men.

Brummer was armed with four powerful 5.9-inch guns, set in single pedestal mounts with splinter shields. One gun was set in front of the fire control tower on the foredeck, one was set on the centre-line of the vessel aft of the bridge superstructure enabling it to fire to either side, and the remaining two were set as a superfiring pair towards the stern. This allowed all four guns to be fired together in a broadside with a range of almost 11 miles. Two 3.4-inch anti-aircraft guns were set between the after funnels and mainmast. She was also fitted with a pair of 20-inch torpedo tubes with four additional torpedoes in a swivel mount amidships.

Brummer and her sister ship *Bremse* were used to successfully raid a British convoy in Norway in October 1917. The two German light cruisers had been constructed in a way that they physically resembled British light cruisers – but to perfect their disguise the two ships, normally in German High Seas Fleet standard light gray, were painted dark gray so they looked even more like British vessels. The subterfuge worked. As the German ships approached the convoy, the British ships flashed recognition signals. The German ships closed unchallenged and then at a range of 2,700 metres opened up with their big 5.9-inch guns, quickly sinking the two escorting destroyers, HMS *Strongbow* and *Mary Rose*. Two armed escort trawlers were then quickly sunk, followed by nine of the 12 ships of the convoy. It was a stunning success.

Brummer was one of eight light cruisers that started to scuttle with the High Seas Fleet in 1919. Of those eight, three were beached and the *Bremse* was subsequently salvaged, but the remaining four: *Dresden*; *Cöln*; *Karlsruhe*; and *Brummer* still lie on the bottom of Scapa Flow.

Today, the wreck of *Brummer* rests in 36 metres of water on her starboard side at position 58° 53.821N, 03° 09.121W. She is therefore completely accessible and is generally in relatively good condition, despite damage in a few places where salvers have carried out blasting and some recent collapsing.

The least depth over her hull is about 20 metres to her upward-facing port side, which is lined with portholes. The 5.9-inch bow deck gun remained *in situ*, defying gravity on the centre-line of the vessel, for more than 80 years until 2003, when it fell from its mount to the seabed. Here it now rests with its barrel pointing slightly upwards. As it tore free of the deck, its weight ripped and buckled the surrounding deck plating and ribs, and this area is now collapsing progressively as the years go by.

Her two masts have fallen to rest on the seabed. They still have their searchlight platforms in place. The forward anchor chains, which would have been run out when she was moored in the Flow before the scuttling, run out from the chain lockers below decks to the circular steam capstans from where they lead out through circular apertures in the deck (the hull hawse pipes).

Immediately behind the fallen 5.9-inch bow gun, sits the fire control tower – with its 3.8-inch thick armour and thin viewing slits ringed round it, some still with their thick glass in place. On top of the fire control tower is a large winged optical range finder. From the greater safety of this armoured fire control tower, the captain and officers would have directed operations while *Brummer* was in battle. The fire control tower along with the whole bridge superstructure collapsed and fell downwards to the seabed in 2010 with some plating falling on top of and partly obscuring the 5.9-inch bow gun on the seabed.

Aft of the collapsed bridge superstructure – and positioned in between the locations of the first and second funnels – is another 5.9-inch gun with splinter shield. The funnels themselves have collapsed to the seabed, leaving ominous black caverns where they once stood that lead down into the bowels of the ship.

The *Brummer* has had extensive blasting carried out by salvers in the vicinity of her engine room and boiler rooms with a large section of the hull blown open. The superimposed deckhouse reforms aft of the blast hole with the main mast running out along the seabed. Her pair of super-firing stern 5.9-inch guns with their splinter shields remain in position on the centre line of the vessel near the stern. Her propellers have been removed at some point in the distant past.

Shipwreck – the essentials

Type of wreck	light cruiser, Bremse class
Nationality	German
Year of construction	1915/6
Dimensions	462 ft x 44 ft x 20 ft
Displacement (tons)	4,308 – design: 5,856 – full load
Date sunk	21 June 1919
Cause of sinking	scuttled
Depth of water	36 metres
Least depth above wreck	20 metres
Position	58 53.821N, 03 09.121W

SMS *Cöln (II)* (Light cruiser, Cöln II class)

Built in Hamburg by Blohm & Voss as *Baunummer* (shipyard registration number) 247, *Cöln (II)* was launched on 5 October 1916, and completed and commissioned into the German Imperial Navy one year later in January 1918, near the end of World War I. She displaced 5,531-tons design and 7,368-tons at combat load. She measured 510 ft in length with a beam of 47 ft and a draft of 21 ft.

She was powered by two sets of coal/oil-fired turbines and twin propellers, which combined to push her to speeds of more than 29 knots. She was protected by 2.4-inch thick main belt armour (along either side) and 0.79 to 1.6-inch thick armour on her deck. The fire control tower, the nerve-centre of the vessel, was protected by thicker 3.8-inch armour. She was heavily armed with eight single 5.9-inch guns on pedestal mounts with splinter shields. Two were set side-by-side on the foredeck in front of the bridge superstructure, one either side of the bridge, one either side of the mainmast, and two superfiring guns on the centre-line near the stern. These guns had a range of almost 11 miles.

Cöln was also fitted with three 3.4-inch anti-aircraft guns situated between the aftmost of her three funnels and the mainmast. In addition to her two submerged 23.6-inch torpedo tubes she boasted eight torpedoes in deck-mounted swivel launchers amidships and a deadly cargo of about 200 mines.

Cöln and her sister *Dresden* were the last light cruisers built by the Kaiserliche Marine and were an improvement on the preceding Königsberg class cruisers. The Cöln class of light cruiser was considerably bigger and more heavily armed than the earlier Bremse class cruisers such as *Brummer*. Designed for a different role they carried more guns but fewer mines. She carried a crew of 559 officers and men.

Completed only 10 months before the end of World War I, her service career was limited. Along with *Dresden* she was assigned to the II Scouting Group of the High Seas Fleet, and with the I Scouting Group and the Second Torpedo-Boat Flotilla on 23–24 April 1918, she participated in an unsuccessful fleet action into the North Sea intended to attack a heavily guarded British convoy to Norway. The group failed to locate the convoy, which had sailed the day before the German Group left port.

Late in the war, in October 1918 *Cöln*, *Dresden* and two other II Scouting Group ships were to attack merchant shipping in the Thames Estuary while the rest of the Group were to bombard targets in Flanders in a coordinated and carefully conceived plan designed to draw out the Royal Navy and lure

Right: The German light cruiser SMS Cöln.

Below: The wreck of the German light cruiser SMS Cöln.

© Rod Macdonald

it into a carefully prepared killing ground where U-boats lurked and mine fields had been laid. It was already clear that the war had been lost and the plan was conceived to inflict as much damage on the Royal Navy as possible to enable Germany to have a stronger negotiating position when it came to peace discussions. It was to be an all or nothing attack whatever the cost to the German Imperial Navy.

On the morning of 29 October 1918 the order was given for the Fleet to sail the following day. Morale amongst the crews was poor – the German sailors were aware that the war was lost and saw little point in throwing away their lives in what was seen as a futile gesture. That night sailors on the *Thüringen* and several battleships mutinied and as the mutiny spread the Kaiser was forced to abandon the plan.

In November 1918, with the Armistice in force, *Cöln* sailed with the rest of the High Seas Fleet for internment at Scapa Flow. On the way there she suffered mechanical problems and fell out of line. Once a leaking condenser had been fixed she completed her journey to Scapa Flow – becoming the last ship of the German line to arrive there.

She sank at Scapa Flow during the scuttle at 1.50 p.m. on 21 June 1919

Today, *Cöln* lies in 35 metres of water on her starboard side at position 58° 53.873N. 03° 08.428W. The least depth over her upward-facing port side is about 20 metres and she is in such good condition that she is regarded as one of the finest dives in the Flow and a wreck that is visited time and time again by divers. She is almost completely intact, barring her forward guns and her propellers, which were salvaged some time ago. Additionally a large hole has been blasted into her towards the stern in the vicinity of her engine rooms and boiler rooms. Rows of portholes line the uppermost port side of her hull.

The bow of the *Cöln* is sleek and narrow and covered with sponges and anemones. The two forward anchor chains rise from chain lockers below decks and run out to circular steam capstans. From here, they run through their hawse pipes in the deck to the side of the vessel where the anchors would once have been held. One chain drops straight down to the seabed, nine metres below, where it is run out for some distance. Twin mooring bollards are set at the side of the hull nearby.

Cöln originally had two 5.9-inch guns with shields in front of her fire control tower towards the bow, but these were salved in the past, leaving only their cogged wracking systems. Immediately aft of the empty gun-mounts the now horizontal oval armoured control tower projects outwards, with its thin viewing slits on two levels ringing completely around it, some slits still with glass in them. On top of the second level of the control tower sits the large winged optical central gun-control range finder. The optics have long since gone, but the scale of it – some eight feet across – is still impressive.

Shipwreck – the essentials	
Type of wreck	light cruiser, Cöln class
Nationality	German
Year of construction	1918
Dimensions	510 ft x 47 ft x 21 ft
Displacement (tons)	5,531 – design: 7,486 – full load
Date sunk	21 June 1919
Cause of sinking	scuttled
Depth of water	36 metres
Least depth above wreck	20 metres
Position	58 53.873N, 03 08.428W

Immediately aft of the control tower, the superstructure and foremast with its cross-rigging and searchlight platforms remains intact, bar a few twisted and burst open plates. The 5.9-inch gun which would have been situated abreast the superstructure on the higher port side has been removed in the past. There is no trace of the three funnels now – they are long since rotted and disintegrated. In their place, large openings some nine feet across in the deck lead down into the bowels of the ship to the thick floor gratings of the next deck level below. On the topmost port side of the hull, empty lifeboat davits hang outwards, their lifeboats having been lowered as the vessel was scuttled.

Just aft of the area where the funnels once stood, abreast the uppermost port side of the mainmast, stands one of the 5.9-inch guns. Its original protective shield is long gone but the barrel still points upwards at an angle towards the distant surface. The raised decking on which this gun-turret stood has corroded away revealing the cylindrical housing for the pedestal's turning mechanism, which runs horizontally towards the main deck.

The mainmast and its large circular platform are set at an angle to the main wreck and mark the start of the largest blasted hole in the wreck, in the engine room area. The hull stops abruptly where the plating has been torn open. The hole is about 12 square metres, and the blurred shape of the hull reforms at the limit of vision.

Just beyond this hole, near the stern, the superimposed 5.9-inch gun and shield set on the raised stern superstructure appears – with its barrel and breech in good condition and encrusted with sea life. Rows of portholes give glimpses into the *Cöln*'s cavernous interior. Just as the extended superimposed gun barrel comes to an end, the superstructure itself ends and on the main deck below sits the aftmost 5.9-inch gun, complete with shield, barrel and breech. Underneath its barrel, the stern anchor capstan is set and the rounded stern of the vessel looms into sight. Mooring bollards and cleats are dotted around the edge of the main deck here.

SMS *Dresden* (Light cruiser, Cöln class)

Built in Kiel by Howaldtswerke, SMS *Dresden* was launched on 25 April 1917, and completed and commissioned into the *Kaiserliche Marine* on 28 March 1918, when she went into service with the German High Seas Fleet. She and her sister Cöln class light cruiser *Cöln (II)* were the last ships

Above: Looking down onto the top of the now horizontal fire control tower © Bob Anderson

Above left: The shield of SMS Dresden *on her starboard bow © Ewan Rowell*

Above right: Bow and twin anchor hawses of SMS Dresden © BobAnderson

commissioned before Germany's defeat in WWI. She displaced 5,531 tons and at full combat load displaced 7,368 tons. Powered by her two sets of coal/oil-fired turbines, her twin propellers could push her to speeds of up to 28 knots, much faster than the 23knots of the battleships of the day. She was 510 feet long with a beam of 47 feet and a draft of almost 20 feet. At a cruising speed of 12 knots she had a range of 5,400 nautical miles

Dresden was protected by 2.4-inch armour plating around her main waterline belt and 0.79 to 1.6-inch thick armour on her deck. Her control tower was more heavily armoured with 3.8-inch thick armour. *Dresden* was fitted with eight powerful 5.9-inch guns in single pedestal mounts with splinter shields and a range of 11 miles. Two were set side-by-side on the foredeck towards the bow, one either side of the bridge, one either side of the mainmast towards the stern, and two superfiring guns set on the centre-line at the stern. She also carried (originally) three 3.4-inch anti-aircraft guns set between her aftmost funnel and her mainmast although one had been removed by the time of her scuttling. She carried four deck-mounted 23.6-inch torpedo tubes: one either side of the foremast and one either side just aft of the aftmost funnel. With her speed and maneuverability she was ideal as a scout for the main fleet, yet she was heavily enough armed that she could fight her way out of trouble with most other surface craft and also target lightly armed merchant shipping. *Dresden* would normally carry about 200 mines and a crew of 559 officers and men.

Being commissioned only eight months before the end of World War I, *Dresden*'s service career was limited and she did not see any direct action. Along with *Cöln (II)* she was assigned to the II Scouting Group and participated in the fleet action to attempt to destroy a heavily guarded British convoy to Norway. The convoy however was not located and the fleet returned to port.

In October 1918 the II Scouting Group was assigned to attack merchant shipping in the Thames estuary and bombard targets in Flanders as part of the last ditch plan to inflict as much damage on the Royal Navy and secure a negotiating position for the peace talks that now appeared inevitable. As the crews of several ships mutinied *Dresden* tried to leave port, however

Above left: The 5.9-inch gun breach and splinter shield on starboard side of the bridge of the SMS Dresden © Ewan Rowell

Above: The German light cruiser SMS Dresden.

the battleship *Markgraf* stood in her way, and trained the 12-inch guns of one of her main armament turrets on her. She then backed down and allowed *Dresden* to leave port. *Dresden* proceeded to Swinemünde where, on hearing that mutinous ships were en route to bombard ships there, she was partially scuttled. When the rumour turned out to be untrue she was refloated and returned to service.

On her arrival with the German High Seas Fleet at Scapa Flow for internment in November 1918, she was moored near the rocky outcrop in the centre of the Flow known as the Barrel of Butter. Once the British discovered that the German fleet was scuttling, the drifter *Clonsin* took

The wreck of the light cruiser SMS Dresden at Scapa Flow with, inset, how she looked in 1989. Note the difference at the foredeck.

© Rod Macdonald

Dresden in tow, even though she was so low in the water that her decks were awash. The progress of the *Clonsin* was made painfully slow by the dead weight of the *Dresden*, which was filling rapidly with water and was low in the sea. The *Clonsin* made for the island of Cava less than a mile away, but on the short journey, *Dresden* continued to flood. When she was about halfway between the Barrel of Butter and Cava, she lurched down by the head and then capsized and sank so quickly that there was no time to cast off the towing cable. She sank at 11.30 a.m. on 21 June 1919.

Shipwreck – the essentials

Type of wreck	light cruiser, Cöln class
Nationality	German
Year of construction	1918
Dimensions	510 ft x 47 ft x 21 ft
Displacement (tons)	5,620 – design: 7,486 – full load
Date sunk	21 June 1919
Cause of sinking	scuttled
Depth of water	34 metres
Least depth above wreck	15 metres
Position	58 52.976N, 03 08.414W

Today the wreck of SMS *Dresden* lies in 34 metres of water at position 58° 52.976N, 03° 08.414W. She rests on her port side with a least depth over her of 16–18 metres at the bow and the stern sitting in deeper water. Being relatively shallow, she has a rich covering of marine growth and entire sections of her, such as the bow, are completely covered in sponges and anemones.

Dresden originally had two side-by-side 5.9-inch guns with shields set on her foredeck, just forward of the bridge superstructure towards the bow. Like the *Cöln*, these were salvaged long ago. On the uppermost starboard side of the hull at the very bow itself, beside the anchor hawse, can be seen a large embossed shield mount, the shield itself having been removed.

In 1995, a gap started to appear between the uppermost starboard side of the hull and the now vertical main deck. After almost 80 years of immersion in seawater, differential corrosion had turned the rivets that held the main deck to the hull, to dust. The deck, free of its restraining rivets, started to fall outwards and downwards. Year by year, the gap between deck and hull got larger and it became progressively unsafe to venture under the overhanging deck.

The deck completed its slow collapse to the seabed in 2000 and now, from the bow to just forward of the fire control tower, the main deck has completely fallen away to leave the large cavernous hull space fully exposed. The internal decks have also long ago rotted away and collapsed to leave nowadays just one large common space.

The bridge superstructure and fire control tower of *Dresden* are fairly intact. The foremast runs out at the back of the bridge from the main deck and although it has fallen to the seabed below, still has its original cross-rigging in place and two circular searchlight platforms. Cables run from various points of the mast to the bridge and deck. At the base of the bridge on the starboard side of the hull one of the main 5.9-inch guns can be found with its barrel facing forward and resting on the superstructure of the bridge beneath it. Steel ladder rungs run up the side of the bridge superstructure to give access to the decks above. Two rows of portholes run along the complete length of the hull.

Aft of the bridge there is a lot of damage – a result of salvaging the condensers and other non-ferrous metal from the engine rooms and boiler rooms. The funnels have rotted away and collapsed and the mainmast is still in place lying on the seabed. Rows of square windows, the glass gone, line the officers' accommodation towards the stern.

The stern in deeper water is relatively intact, with both super-firing 5.9-inch guns still in place. Just before the aftmost 5.9-inch gun, in the aft facing superimposed deckhouse wall, a now horizontal doorway allows easy access into the officers' accommodation and a swim through of more than 50 feet. The stern anchor still sits in its hawse.

SMS *Karlsruhe* (Light cruiser, Königsberg II class)

Built at Wilhelmshaven by Kaiserliches Werft, the Königsberg II class light cruiser *Karlsruhe* was laid down in 1915, launched on 31 January 1916 and commissioned into the German High Seas Fleet on 15 November 1916. Driven by two coal/oil-fired turbines, her two propellers could push her to speeds of nearly 28 knots. She was protected by a 2.4-inch thick layer of armour plating on her main belt and on her deck. Her fire control tower had a 3.8-inch layer of protective armour plating.

She carried eight 5.9-inch guns in single pedestal mounts with splinter shields. Of these, two were set side-by-side on the foredeck towards the bow: two were set one either side of the bridge facing forward, two faced astern on either side and just forward of the mainmast, and two were set astern in a superfiring position on the centre-line of the vessel. There were two 3.5-inch anti-aircraft guns mounted between the aftmost funnel and the main mast and two 19.7-inch deck-mounted torpedo tubes. She could carry 200 mines. She had an operational crew complement of 475 officers and men, and had a range of 4,850 nautical miles.

The Cöln class light cruisers *Cöln* and *Dresden* had their heavily armoured control towers incorporated into the superstructure of the bridge. This facilitated better communications with the crew and gave the ability for officers to get up to the higher observation platform quickly. The earlier *Brummer* and *Karlsruhe* had a markedly different arrangement, where the fire control tower was set on the main deck some distance forward of the bridge superstructure, making it a small, well-armoured target. If an enemy scored a direct hit on the bridge, the armoured control tower would be unaffected. This location however was found to have poor visibility in combat due to the smoke from the forward guns.

On 16 August 1917, *Karlsruhe* participated in a minesweeping operation in the North Sea. She was part of an escort for minesweepers clearing Route Yellow, one of the channels in the minefields used by U-boats to leave and return to port. Lookouts on one of the minesweepers spotted a British

Shipwreck – the essentials	
Type of wreck	light cruiser, Königsberg II class
Nationality	German
Year of construction	1916
Dimensions	497 ft x 47 ft x 20 ft
Displacement (tons)	5,540 – design: 7,125 – full load
Date sunk	21 June 1919
Cause of sinking	scuttled
Depth of water	24 metres
Least depth above wreck	12 metres
Position	58 53.388N, 03 11.282W

squadron of three light cruisers and sixteen destroyers approaching. The minesweepers fled south under cover of smoke screens and the British ships broke off their attack. *Karlsruhe* and the rest of the escort failed to come to their aid, however, and the commander of the operation was subsequently relieved of command.

In early September 1917, following the German conquest of the Russian port of Riga, the German navy decided to eliminate the Russian naval forces that still held the Gulf of Riga and set up Operation Albion to seize the Baltic island of Ösel and the Russian gun batteries on the Sworbe peninsula. The battlecruiser *Moltke*, along with the III and IV Battle Squadrons of the High Seas Fleet and an invasion force of some 24,600 troops was gathered. *Karlsruhe* and the rest of the II Scouting Group would provide the cruiser screen for the naval task force.

On the morning of 12 October, the operation began with *Moltke* and the III Squadron ships engaging Russian shore positions in Tagga Bay while IV Squadron shelled Russian gun batteries on the Sworbe

Left: Forward anchor capstans on SMS Karlsruhe © Ewan Rowell

Far left: The German light cruiser SMS Karlsruhe.

Below: The wreck of the German light cruiser SMS Karlsruhe.

© Rod Macdonald

peninsula. On 18/19 October, *Karlsruhe* and the II Scouting Group covered minesweepers operating off the island of Dagö. By 20 October, the islands were under German control and the Russian naval forces had either been destroyed or forced to withdraw. The German ships were subsequently ordered back to the North Sea.

In October 1918, *Karlsruhe* and elements of the II Scouting Group were to lead the final all or nothing attack on the British navy with a bombardment of targets in Flanders whilst the rest of II Scouting Group including *Cöln* and *Dresden* targeted merchant shipping in the Thames estuary. The plan was to draw the Royal Navy out to a prepared killing zone and inflict significant damage in order to secure a better bargaining position for Germany, whatever the cost to the fleet. As crews on ships mutinied at this seemingly futile gesture the unrest ultimately forced the operation to be cancelled.

A month later, *Karlsruhe* steamed into internment at Scapa Flow with the rest of the High Seas Fleet. Seven long months later, on 21 June 1919, she sank at anchor in the Flow at 3.50 p.m.

Today the wreck of the *Karlsruhe* lies in roughly 26 metres of water off the northerly tip of Cava (with its conspicuous white lighthouse) at position 58° 53.388N, 03° 11.282W. She rests on her starboard side and is a shallower dive than the *Dresden*, *Brummer* or *Cöln*. She is often used as a shakedown dive at the beginning of a week's diving, allowing divers to experience Scapa Flow diving and a German WWI wreck in relatively shallow water. She has a least depth over her of about 12–14 metres. There is a four-metre difference in depth between the bottom on the keel side and the deeper deck side, presumably as a result of scouring or a sloping bottom.

Unlike the other light cruisers, she is heavily damaged as a result of extensive blasting by salvers. Being a Königsberg II class light cruiser, built early in World War I in 1915, she was fitted out to a high specification. (The Cöln class cruisers *Cöln* and *Dresden* were built towards the end of the war when non-ferrous metals were running short and so were built of poorer quality metals). The entire bridge superstructure was made of

½-inch brass plate and weighed 4½ tons. It was blasted off and lifted to the surface intact in one section in the 1970s.

As a result of salvage blasting (to remove the forward non-ferrous submerged torpedo tubes) and the consequent collapse of the bow, the two side-by-side foredeck 5.9-inch guns have collapsed downwards - with the lower now lying on the seabed. The fire control tower and detached foremast lie nearby. The aft-facing armoured door of the fire control tower itself is missing, allowing a glimpse inside. The door fell from its mount in the 1990s, trapping an unfortunate diver passing underneath by the leg and pinning him to the seabed as it landed. Thankfully, a fellow diver was able to help lift the heavy armoured door enough to let him free. The two forward anchor capstans sit almost on top of each other in amongst the collapsed debris of the bow. The starboard anchor chain lies run out on the seabed for some distance, lying as it fell when the vessel sank during the scuttling. The anchor itself is well embedded in the silt at its end.

The uppermost port side of her hull is now almost horizontal and the deck, with its original wood planking still visible in places, sits almost vertically at right angles to the seabed. A pronounced bilge keel (about a metre high) juts out from the hull and runs for some distance along the keel. The blasting to recover the non-ferrous bow torpedo tubes in the 1970's blew open a candle locker and hundreds of candles in first-class condition bearing the legend, '*Kaiserliche Marine*', floated out from it.

The ship loses its shape where the entire bridge superstructure has been removed but aft of there the hull reforms. The three funnels are long collapsed and rotted away leaving large openings into the hull.

The hull has been opened up at the engine room area towards the stern and in this area there is a tangle of torn plating and mechanical parts. Parts of the turbines can be seen, their non-ferrous individually keyed blades now a purple colour.

The 5.9-inch guns abreast the main mast and the super-firing pair at the stern, have been removed. At the very stern, although her propellers are

Top: The stern and anchor of SMS Karlsruhe © Bob Anderson

Above: Aft deck anchor capstan. SMS Karlsruhe © Bob Anderson

missing, her kedge anchor, still on its chain, has slipped from its hawse and fallen to the seabed. The plating of the hull bottom at the stern has rotted through to leave a latticework of structural ribs and frames through which it is possible to swim.

THE 15-INCH GUN-TURRETS OF THE BATTLESHIP *BAYERN*

The battleship *Bayern* was the latest in state-of-the-art warship construction when she came into service in the German High Seas Fleet in 1916 as the lead ship of the Bayern class of battleships. She was laid down in January 1914, launched in February 1915 and entered service in July 1916 – too late by just two weeks to fight at the Battle of Jutland. The original intention was that she would form the nucleus of a Fourth Battle Squadron in the High Seas Fleet, along with three other planned sister battleships, *Baden, Sachsen* and *Württemberg.* However, only one of the other planned three ships, *Baden,* was completed. The other two were cancelled later in the war, when materials and production requirements focused on U-boat construction.

Bayern was 591 ft long with a beam of 99 ft and a draft of 31 ft. Her design displacement was 29,080 tons and fully loaded for combat she displaced 31,690 tons. Her main vertical armour belt along either side was 14.5 inches thick. She had a range of 5,000 miles at 12 knots and, driven by her three Parsons turbines, which developed 48,000 shp (shaft horsepower), she had a top speed of 22 knots. She carried a crew of 42 officers and 1,129 men.

Bayern was the first German ship to be fitted with eight powerful 15-inch guns set in four twin turrets, replacing the 12-inch guns of the earlier classes. Two super-firing turrets were set on the centre-line of the vessel in front of the conning tower and superstructure. The other two turrets were again set as a super-firing pair towards the stern.

Her secondary armament consisted of sixteen 5.9-inch guns – the standard main gun on the light cruisers, six 3.45-inch guns and five 23.6-inch underwater torpedo tubes – set one in the bow and two on each side of the ship.

Commissioned so late in World War I, her service career was limited. She joined the III Battle Squadron of the High Seas Fleet on 15 July 1916. Her then wireless operator was a certain Ernst Lindemann, who would go on to command the battleship *Bismarck* as it broke out into the Atlantic during WWII – and was ultimately sunk.

In August 1916 an operation to draw out and destroy Admiral David Beatty's battlecruisers was to begin with a bombardment of British coastal towns by the I Scouting Group. *Moltke* and *Von der Tann* were the only German battlecruisers still in fighting condition after the Battle of Jutland and so three dreadnought battleships were assigned to the operation, *Bayern* and the two König class battleships *Markgraf* and *Grosser Kurfürst*. The remainder of the High Seas Fleet, including some 15 capital ships, would follow up to the rear and provide cover.

The British code breakers however had already broken German codes and were aware of the planned operation - the main British Grand Fleet was sortied to confront the German force. Admiral Reinhard Scheer in charge of the German fleet was warned of the Grand Fleet's approach and, unwilling to risk his fleet so soon after the bloody losses at Jutland, he turned his ships around and retreated to the German base.

Bayern was involved in another sortie into the North Sea on 18-20 October 1916 – which did not contact British naval forces.

In September 1917 she was assigned as part of the naval force to take part in Operation Albion – the conquest of the Russian-held Baltic islands in the Gulf of Riga. The force consisted of the flagship *Moltke* and III Battle Squadron, the V Division which consisted of *Bayern* and the four König class battleships and the VI Division of five Kaiser class battleships. With supporting light cruisers, torpedo-boat flotillas and dozens of mine warfare ships, the entire naval force amounted to more than 300 ships. More than 100 aircraft and 6 zeppelins gave air support to the invasion force, which amounted to some 24,600 men. Russian forces opposing this mighty German force consisted of a couple of old Russian pre-dreadnoughts, several dated and vulnerable armoured cruisers, 26

Bayern *turrets.*

© Rod Macdonald

destroyers and an assortment of torpedo boats and smaller gunboats. The Russian garrison on the islands amounted to some 14,000 men.

The attack began on 12 October when, in a move designed to secure the channel between the Moon and Dagö islands, *Bayern*, *Moltke* and the four König's began firing on Russian shore batteries at Tagga Bay whilst the five Kaiser class battleships simultaneously bombarded the Russian shore batteries on the Sworbe peninsula. Successful control of this channel would block the only route of escape for the Russian ships in the Gulf of Riga itself.

Just after the attack had begun, at 0507, *Bayern* struck a mine as she moved to her bombardment position at Pamerot. The explosion killed 7 of her crew and subsequent flooding caused her bow to settle by 2 metres. Despite the damage she still engaged the naval battery at Cape Toffri before being released from her duties for repair nine hours later at 1400. Temporary local repairs proved problematic and she had to be withdrawn from the operation and sent to the naval shipyards at Kiel for repair.

A year later, after the Armistice of November 1918 had halted the fighting, *Bayern* steamed into internment at Scapa Flow with the rest of the High Seas Fleet. Seven months later, she sank with the Fleet at 2.30 p.m. on 21 June 1919.

After languishing on the bottom of Scapa Flow for 14 years, in June 1933, Metal Industries Ltd started to prepare the massive submerged battleship for lifting to the surface. When divers inspected her they found that she, like the other battleships, had turned turtle as she sank because of the enormous weight of her turrets, conning tower and superstructure bearing her over to one side as seawater flooded in. She lay with the flat bottom of her hull facing upwards and much of her superstructure embedded in the seabed beneath.

During the course of the salvage operations, a compressed air hosepipe burst inside the hull – and the sunken battleship started to overfill with compressed air. The ship gradually became buoyant and eventually broke free of the suction of the seabed and started to rise to the surface. The four massive twin 15-inch gun-turrets, underneath the upturned ship, had not yet been secured for lifting. They broke free from their mounts and were left upside down on the seabed.

Once on the surface, air started to escape from the hull. *Bayern* slowly became negatively buoyant and sank to the seabed again – this time, moved on the surface by the current, in a slightly different position.

After three further months of painstaking work, *Bayern* was finally ready for a controlled ascent. This time everything went according to plan. *Bayern* lifted off the seabed and rose to the surface amidst frothing eruptions of white water at her sides as expanding air escaped from her.

Today, the four massive twin 15-inch gun turrets of the *Bayern* remain upside down on the seabed in a line, marking where the ship lay after the scuttling – and before its first unexpected journey to the surface. The business part of the turrets – the Gun Rooms that housed the massive breaches of the 15-inch guns – were protected by 14 inches of armour plating. Each turret had a revolving weight of 1020 tons.

The turrets are grouped in pairs, the aft two superfiring turrets to the southeast and the forward superfiring pair to the northwest. The two pairs of turrets are separated by a gap of some 100 metres and lie in a 4-metre deep depression – the outline of where the ship lay on the seabed before it was lifted. A second less marked depression marks where the ship came to rest on the seabed after it sunk again. The second depression shows that the forward part of the ship actually sank onto the forward pair of turrets, which still lay on the seabed.

In German ships, a Gunnery Officer in the *fore control* was in charge of the guns. The fore control was an armoured chamber, which formed the rear portion of the conning tower and from which the vessel's captain, supported by the navigating officer and the signal officer navigated the ship in action. The Gunnery Officer had a number of officers and about 750 men under his control all dedicated to the process of firing – in action, almost half the crew were allocated in some way to the guns. The Gunnery Officer was supported by three lower ranking gunnery officers, who controlled the secondary battery, by men on the range finder, men on the director and a number for transmitting orders. Immediately below and often separated only by an iron grating on which they stood, more messengers stood waiting. In all there would be more than 30 men in the fore control – which was armoured sufficiently to withstand a hit from a 6-inch gun at short range.

The secondary gunnery officer had his post in the *after control* and observers for the fall of shot on the enemy were stationed in the spotting top some 35 metres up the foremast.

All orders from the gunnery officers went by telephone or speaking tube to transmitting stations situated well below the waterline at the bottom of the ship where they were protected by the armour belt and bunkers. From there, orders and information were transmitted to individual guns.

The upper part of the main turret, the Gun Room, consisted of a heavily armoured revolving turret, turned by electricity, and the revolving platform on which the guns were situated. The ammunition hoists, through which shells were passed from the magazines below to the Transfer Room and thence to the Gun Room (inside the shelter of the armoured cylindrical barbette), also turned as the turret revolved. Behind the guns was a relay of ammunition, about 6 rounds for each gun.

The revolving turret rotated on the fixed armoured barbette, which was some 30–40 feet wide and was integral to the structure of the ship. The barbette reached down through several deck levels to the armoured deck at its base. The interior of this barbette was divided into several tiers – the Transfer Room, the Switch Room, the magazine and the cartridge magazine. In all, including the Gun Room of the turret, the barbette was some 5 stories high and housed 70–80 men – a total of some 350 men in all four turrets.

The function of the Transfer Room was to send ammunition up to the

The battleship Bayern *goes down by the stern. C.W. Burrows*

guns. There were no hoists running right through from the magazine below to the turret in the German ships that would be vulnerable to the flash from an explosion reaching all the way down to the magazine. The magazine and cartridge ammunition hoists connected to an intermediate station, the Transfer Room. The transfer procedure delayed the process of sending the shell or cartridge from the magazine to the gun – but two rounds of cartridges for each gun were simultaneously on their way at all times. Only a small stock of ammunition and cartridges was kept in the Transfer Room and thus it – not the magazine – became the reservoir from which the gun was supplied.

German guns could fire comfortably with both guns in a twin turret every 30 seconds. If a greater rate of fire was required, they could fire a single gun from each turret every 15 seconds. They would often fire a salvo of four single shells, one from each turret, every 20 seconds.

The Germans held their primary cartridge powder in brass cases. The 6-inch cartridge looked exactly like a giant sporting cartridge. These large brass cases were difficult to manufacture, were expensive and extremely heavy – but notwithstanding these drawbacks the German navy used these brass cases even for the heaviest calibres. This practice saved them for catastrophes such as the magazine explosions of HMS *Indefatigable*, *Queen Mary*, *Invincible* and the older armoured cruisers at the Battle of Jutland. The powder required for a large calibre main gun could not all be contained in a brass case – so in addition the Germans used a secondary cartridge, the powder for which was contained in a double silk pouch. These naturally caught fire easier than the brass cases. The British kept all their powder in silk pouches, which were thought to represent a considerable saving in weight and magazine space compared to brass cartridge cases.

The Germans kept all those cartridges, which were not by the gun or on the ammunition hoists, in tin canisters so that they could not easily catch fire. With a view to minimizing the dangers of a flash fire and catastrophic explosion, German orders were that only one secondary and one main cartridge were to be kept on the platform by each gun, and the same rule applied on the lower tiers of the platform.

The upturned turrets of *Bayern* lie in 38 metres of water, not far from *Kronprinz Wilhelm*, and are well settled into the silty seabed. The turret Gun Rooms and the barrels of the guns themselves are buried in the silt and cannot be seen – although the outline of parts of the base of the turrets can be made out in places. The Gun Rooms are large rooms beneath the level of the seabed and glimpses down into them can be made in a number of places through parts of the ammunition host machinery, some openings being large enough for a diver to enter the Gun Room with care and inspect the massive breaches.

The turrets turned on 6-inch diameter ball-bearings in a ball race which still rings around the outside rim of the circular turning mechanism. The vertical cylindrical armoured barbettes, which took the weight of the turrets and on which the turrets turned, being an integral part of the structure of the ship, went up to the surface with the ship when it was lifted. Today, what is left on the seabed sticking up from the buried Gun Rooms is the turret turning mechanism and the ammunition hoist apparatus – which turned with the turret inside the barbette.

The turning mechanism and hoists on the southmost pair of turrets rise up vertically some 14 metres to a depth of about 24 metres. When *Bayern* sank for the second time, turned by the tide to a slightly different angle the hull landed on the northmost pair of turrets and consequently the machinery and apparatus on these two does not rise up so high.

In the illustration, the four turrets can be seen in line astern along the massive depression in the seabed that reveals *Bayern*'s first resting place. The second depression lies at an oblique angle towards the top of the illustration. In between the two sets of turrets in the depression lie sections of the mainmast and the foremast. The foremast spotting top sits in the depression near the turrets, at the top of the illustration.

In 2011, the author and Paul Haynes led a rope from one set of turrets to the distant set, making it possible for divers to follow the depression from one set of turrets to the other.

Shipwreck – the essentials	
Type of wreck	Bayern class battleship
Nationality	German
Year of construction	1914/16
Dimensions	591 ft x 98.5 ft x 31 ft
Displacement (tons)	28,080 – design: 31,700 – full load
Date sunk	21 June 1919
Cause of sinking	scuttled
Depth of water	38 metres
Least depth above wreck	24 metres
Position	
East pair of turrets	58 53.919N, 03 10.602W
West pair of turret	58 53.926N, 03 10.675W

THE ICELANDIC TRAWLER JAMES BARRIE

The *James Barrie* was a 666-grt Hull steam trawler originally known as the *Benella*, registration no. H15. She was built in Aberdeen in 1949 and was 180.5 ft long with a beam of 30.4 ft.

On 27 March 1969 the *James Barrie* was passing through the Pentland Firth on her way from Hull to the Icelandic fishing grounds. At about 8 p.m., she ran hard aground on the Louther Rock: one of the dangerous collection of four uninhabited islands known as the Pentland Skerries, which lie about halfway across the Pentland Firth between Duncansby Head and the

Right: A diver peers into the wheelhouse of the James Barrie © Ewan Rowell

Far right: The Hull trawler James Barrie.

Below: The James Barrie.

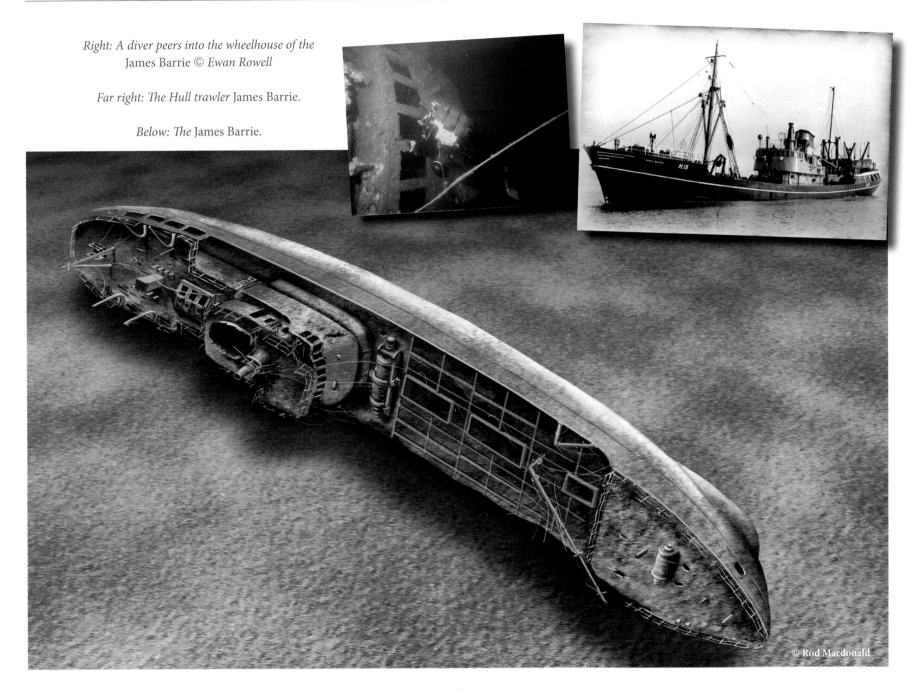

© Rod Macdonald

Top: The wheelhouse of the James Barrie *© Bob Anderson*

Above: Port side of the James Barrie *© Bob Anderson*

south-most Orkney island of South Ronaldsay. The Louther Rock lies about one mile from the largest of these rocky islands, Muckle Skerry, which has a small lighthouse on it.

The *James Barrie* was stuck fast on the south-east side of the Louther Skerry. Her hull had been holed on her port bow and she started to take on water heavily. Her stern was well up and she heeled over to her port side.

The 70-foot Kirkwall lifeboat *Grace Paterson Ritchie* and the Wick lifeboat were called out, the *Grace Paterson Ritchie* arriving on scene at 10.45 p.m. The *James Barrie*'s crew had got their lifeboats (swung in davits at the stern) ready for lowering, and although in no immediate danger, they were ready to abandon ship if the situation got worse. As High Water would be at 8 a.m. the next morning, it was hoped that an attempt could be made to float her off the rocks at that time. The two lifeboats stood by the stricken vessel all through the night in case of trouble.

During the night, the wind rose and conditions worsened. As the tide started to rise, the *James Barrie* began to rock back and forth, her keel almost afloat. She was however leaking badly and at 6.05 a.m., water started coming into the engine room and the skipper was forced to give the order to abandon ship. The crew of 21 lowered their two lifeboats and clambered into them – the Wick lifeboat then came close in and picked them up.

The *James Barrie* remained stranded on the Louther Skerry for the next two days. Then, on 29 March, she slid off and floated away unmanned on the tide into the Pentland Firth. She was spotted adrift by the Pentland Skerries lighthouse keepers when she was a mile or so away. The Kirkwall lifeboat, *Grace Paterson Ritchie,* was called out once again and took the *James Barrie* in tow, stern first to avoid forcing more water in through her damaged bow. Pumps were set up onboard to get rid of as much water as possible from inside her hull as the tow made for Scapa Pier in Scapa Bay, just to the south of Kirkwall. The *James Barrie*, however, was shipping more water than the pumps could handle and after being towed more than nine miles – almost halfway along its slow journey to Scapa – she rolled over onto her starboard side and sank less than a minute later.

She now lies in Hoxa Sound, off Widewall Bay, about a mile south of Hoxa Head.

Shipwreck – the essentials	
Type of wreck	Icelandic trawler
Nationality	British
Year of construction	1949
Dimensions	180.5 ft x 30.4 ft
Tonnage	666-grt
Date sunk	29 March 1969
Cause of sinking	grounding
Depth of water	42 metres
Least depth above wreck	35 metres
Position	58 48.780N, 03 02.201W

Today, the 181-foot-long *James Barrie* lies on her starboard side in 42 metres of water on a clean, sandy bottom at position 58º 48.780N, 03º 02.201ºW. The least depth over her is about 35 metres. The vessel is practically intact, save for her large bronze propeller, which was salved in the 1980s. Unlike the German wrecks inside the Flow where there is little current, this wreck lies in the main channel into Scapa Flow – Hoxa Sound – and is heavily affected by the tide. She can only be dived at Slack Water. The strong tides do however have a benefit, as they regularly sweep Hoxa Sound clear of any silt or sediment. The *James Barrie* is renowned for its crystal clear visibility, which regularly is 20 metres or more. The bow is a majestic sight and still has her anchor winch set on the fo'c'stle deck and guardrails ringing around its top. Dropping from the fo'c'stle to the now

The wheelhouse of the James Barrie
© *Bob Anderson*

vertical main deck, the hatches for the fish and ice holds can still be made out in amongst the skeletal framework of her now exposed structure. Her mast has fallen down to the seabed at an oblique angle.

Just in front of the wheelhouse a large winch sits on the deck with trawl wires still wrapped around it. The classic Icelandic trawler wheelhouse behind is ringed with square windows, the glass long gone, but which allow glimpses inside. A doorway on the port side lies open, the door itself is missing. The funnel has rotted and collapsed to the seabed.

Aft of the wheelhouse superstructure, on the Boat Deck, the pitched roof of the engine room allows glimpses in through open skylights. Behind it a

Above left: The F 2.

Above: The wreck of the F 2 *in Gutter Sound with barge YC 21 in the background.*

raised companionway doorway faces aft in between the now empty lifeboat davits – a silent reminder of the drama of her sinking.

THE ESCORT VESSEL *F 2* & THE SALVAGE BARGE *YC 21*

The *F 2* was a German World War II escort vessel (*Geleiteboot*), similar to a destroyer. She was laid down as the second of a class of ten such vessels at the Germaniawerft shipyard in Kiel in 1934 and was completed in 1936. Measuring 249 ft in length with a beam of 29 ft and a draft of 11 ft, she displaced 790 tons.

The *F 2* was used as an experimental ship, and in 1938/39 in the run up to WWII her length was increased to 263 ft and her displacement reduced to 756 tons. At this time she was converted to a torpedo recovery vessel and her four 37mm anti-aircraft guns were removed leaving her with four 20mm anti-aircraft guns set in two twin mounts. She was equipped with two large single 4.1-inch guns with shields, set one on the bow and one to the stern.

Driven by twin Brown-Boveri turbines and two propellers, she developed 14,000-shp (shaft horse-power) and could achieve speeds of about 28 knots prior to her lengthening in 1939, when her speed was reduced to about 26 knots. The design was essentially experimental and her high-pressure boilers proved problematic. She carried a crew of 121 officers and men.

F 2 was handed over to Britain at the end of World War II by way of reparations and was moored in Gutter Sound, where she sank at her moorings a year later in 1946, not far from the British naval base at Lyness.

Today, the *F 2* lies only about half a mile from

Lyness in Gutter Sound, where many of the dive-boats stop for lunch after the morning dive. Being shallower than the German Fleet and close to Lyness, she makes a good second or afternoon dive. She lies at position 58° 50.778°N, 03° 11.521°W in 16–18 metres of water, on her port side, and has a least depth to her hull of about eight metres. The bow to aft of the bridge is intact and in good condition. From the bridge to the stern, however, the vessel has been devastated by blasting and is hardly recognisable – a mass of tangled pipes, cables, plates and debris.

At the bow, mooring bollards are dotted around the edge of the deck. The winch on her forward deck still holds a reel of steel cable. Her anchor chains are run out from her anchor chain lockers to circular steam-driven capstans and out through their hawse pipes to hang down to the seabed. Just in front of the bridge superstructure, the impressive 4.1-inch gun looms into view, the barrel still pointing directly ahead. The open back of the gun shield reveals the breech and working mechanism of the gun.

Just behind the 4.1-inch gun, there is an open deck-hatch, with its access

Shipwreck – the essentials

F 2

Type of wreck	escort vessel
Nationality	German
Year of construction	1936
Dimensions	262 ft x 28.9 ft x 10.6 ft
Displacement (tons)	790
Date sunk	30 December 1946
Cause of sinking	storm
Depth of water	16 metres
Least depth above wreck	8 metres
Position	58° 50.778°N, 03° 11.521°W?

Shipwreck – the essentials

YC 21

Type of wreck	barge
Nationality	British
Year of construction	
Dimensions	
Displacement (tons)	
Date sunk	15 November 1968
Cause of sinking	storm
Depth of water	16 metres
Least depth above wreck	10 metres

ladder still in place, leading into the depths of the bow. The foremast, which originally ran out from the top of the bridge behind, has fallen onto the seabed below – it is still intact and has a searchlight platform on it, now half buried in the silty bottom.

Amidships in the blasted area, the hull loses its shape completely, but on the seabed to starboard, about six metres east of the main wreckage, lies what looks like the cogged wracking system for one of her anti-aircraft guns. At her stern, the propeller-shaft and bearings can still be seen, but the propeller itself has been salvaged.

F 2 was purchased in 1967 by Metrec Engineering, 'to be blown up and salvaged'. It seems that they had made quite a decent job of it before another piece of Scapa Flow history would be written – for about 50 metres away from the bow section of *F 2* lies the 550-ton wooden barge *YC 21*. It sank in a storm on 15 November 1968, ironically while it was being used in salvage operations on *F 2*. In its hold can still be found one of the *F 2*'s twin 20-millimetre anti-aircraft guns – lifted and stowed before *YC 21* sank.

YC 21 makes an excellent second dive in her own right – but lying so close to *F 2*, the two wrecks are often combined into one dive. After exploring *F 2*, divers can navigate back to the keel of the bow section. Where the keel loses its shape and gives way to the blasted stern section, a guide rope is usually fixed running out across a silty gap, which is strewn with bottles and crockery. Following this rope, very soon the hull of *YC 21* appears out of the gloom – sitting on an even keel.

YC 21 is small enough to easily explore in one dive. She is a wooden-hulled vessel, her planks held in place by copper spikes with identification markings on them. In places, the planks have sprung or rotted away, allowing glimpses into her innards. Underneath the twin 20-millimetre anti-aircraft gun in the main hold lies another single-barreled gun. At the very back of this hold, a row of lockers and a workbench can be made out. A passageway leads aft from here down a corridor and opens out into a completely enclosed stern room.

THE BOOM-DEFENCE VESSEL HMT *STRATHGARRY*

HMT (His Majesty's Trawler) *Strathgarry* was a 202-grt single-deck steam trawler built in Aberdeen in 1906 by Hay, Russell & Co. Ltd – her official number being 123363. She had a length of 113 ft, a beam of 21.9 ft and a draft of 11.7 ft. Her single screw was driven by a three-cylinder triple-expansion engine built in Aberdeen by Hay, Russell & Co., which produced 67 horsepower (net). She was registered in Aberdeen as A97 and initially owned by the Aberdeen Steam Trawling & Fishing Co. Ltd.

After World War I had started, she was requisitioned for the Royal Navy in June 1915, and after conversion, was put to use as a boom-defence vessel. Although the Sounds, the channels into Scapa Flow, had been blocked by the sinking of blockships, the main channel into the Flow – Hoxa Sound – had to remain navigable to allow Royal Navy vessels to enter and leave. Precautions however had to be taken to protect the warships of the British Grand Fleet inside the great naval anchorage – Scapa Flow had to be made impregnable.

To prevent U-boats getting into Scapa Flow through Hoxa Sound, anti-submarine nets or 'booms' were strung right across it at strategic places, suspended from large floats and weighed down to a few feet above the seabed by heavy concrete weights. A way – or door – had to be left in the boom to allow British vessels in and out of the anchorage. Boom-defence vessels would patrol the boom and open and close a section of the boom as friendly vessels passed through. A watchful eye had to be kept for signs of any U-boat that might try to slip through the boom at this vulnerable time by following closely behind a British ship.

Shipwreck – the essentials	
Type of wreck	boom-defence vessel (steam trawler)
Nationality	British
Year of construction	1906
Dimensions	113 ft x 21.9 ft x 11.7 ft
Tonnage	202-grt
Date sunk	6 July 1915
Cause of sinking	collision
Depth of water	58 metres
Least depth above wreck	52 metres
Position	58° 49.71N, 003° 02.95W

Just weeks after taking up her duties at Scapa Flow, on 6 July 1915, HMT *Strathgarry* was sunk in a deep part of Hoxa Sound following a collision with the 581 foot long, 25,870-ton Orion class battleship HMS *Monarch*, as the 2nd Battle Squadron of the Grand Fleet was entering Scapa Flow. In the turmoil of the war, such a small vessel, with nothing of any great value worth salvaging from her in such depths, was soon forgotten about. The wreck was located in 1974 and on 23 July 1975 it was swept by HMS *Herald* and reported as clear to the maximum sweep depth of 35 metres. Sport divers first starting visiting her in the 1980's.

Top right: The stump of the mast of HMT Strathgarry on the after deck with an Admiralty pattern anchor and stock still lashed in place on the deck © Ewan Rowell

The wreck of the boom-defence vessel HMT Strathgarry rests in 60 metres of water in Hoxa Sound.

© Rod Macdonald

The wreck of HMT *Strathgarry* today sits on her keel with a pronounced list to port in 58 metres of water in Hoxa Sound at 58° 49.71N, and 03° 02.95W. There is a least depth over her of 52 metres and being in such deep water she is a wreck only for technical divers using mixed gases in place of compressed air. Being situated in Hoxa Sound, the main channel in and out of the Flow, the seabed is swept clean of any silt by the fierce tides and this produces beautiful 20-metre underwater visibility, similar to the wreck of the trawler *James Barrie* which lies about one mile away. These same tides, however, mean that this wreck has to be dived at Slack Water.

The wreck sits on clean white sand and shale, and at only 113 ft in length, can easily be fully explored in one dive, despite the constrictions placed on the diver by the depth. Practically all her wooden deck planking has now rotted away, leaving only small pieces visible above the latticework of her structure. The foredeck has collapsed down and prominently shelves off to port – perhaps evidence of where the 25,870-ton HMS *Monarch* struck her in 1915 and sent her to the bottom.

Four large cable winches used for operations with the anti-submarine boom sit on her foredeck with their cables still neatly coiled around them. Just aft of this stands the open skeletal framework of the wheelhouse with the hub of the helm, with it spokes radiating out, still standing in place. Just behind the helm stood the brass rudder direction-indicator, with its embossed lettering and pointer.

Aft of the wheelhouse, a large black hole marks where the funnel formerly stood. Aft of that, the rotting skeleton of a wide deckhouse can be explored, with its two entrance doors facing astern – the door of one still fully opened back against the bulkhead. The afterdeck planking has rotted away, exposing the beams and frames of her structure. Remnants of the wooden deck planks, just a few inches wide are still evident up and down the structural steel frames where metallic salts have leached from the frames into the surrounding wood. The metallic salts have forced the shipworms and other woodborers consuming the decking to stop at the contaminated wood. If there is one thing that leaves a horrid taste in a woodborer's mouth, it is anything metallic.

The stub of her main mast stands just aft of this deckhouse and aft of that a spare anchor some 2-3 metres long lies athwartships, still neatly stowed in place with its stock folded away alongside it and lashed down in shipshape fashion. Abruptly, the blunt stern appears with the auxiliary steering mechanism still discernible. Peering over the bulwark rail, the rudder and propeller can easily be made out below in the good visibility.

THE ARMOURED CRUISER HMS *HAMPSHIRE*

The name of one of Britain's greatest war heroes, Lord Kitchener, will forever be linked with Orkney. For it was here, off the bleak 200-foot-high cliffs of Marwick Head on the west coast, that the 10,850-ton armoured cruiser HMS *Hampshire*, carrying Lord Kitchener on a voyage to Russia, struck a mine and sank. At 450 ft long, the *Hampshire* was a strong, powerful warship, well suited to the ill-fated voyage through the colossal seas around the north cape of Norway to the port of Archangel in northern Russia. But of the crew of 655 and Lord Kitchener and his staff, only 12 would survive.

The wreck of HMS *Hampshire* lies in 70 metres of water 1.5 miles off Marwick Head, where high on its desolate cliffs the tall, solitary Kitchener Memorial marks the nearest land point to the site of the sinking.

Lord Kitchener had been the driving force behind Britain's recruitment campaign in the early years of World War I with his famous 'YOUR COUNTRY NEEDS YOU' poster. By 1916, the hand of fate had turned against him and he was being openly criticised for his war tactics and beliefs. In the years following his death, a bitter controversy raged about the sinking. Was it really a mine, as per the official explanation – or was it a bomb planted by German, Irish or even British saboteurs? Great play was made of the fact that the Stromness lifeboat had not put to sea to pick up survivors, and that locals trying to get to the scene to help in a shore-search were turned back at bayonet point.

© Rod Macdonald

The wreck of HMS Hampshire rests in 68 metres of water off Marwick Head to the north west of Orkney.

Russian ineptitude in organising their own affairs and the vast sums of money being expended by Britain in funding the Russian war effort resulted in the decision to send Lord Kitchener to Russia, to impress on the Russians that Britain was not a bottomless fund of munitions and to discuss common war aims and strategy.

At the beginning of June 1916, Kitchener travelled up to Thurso and crossed the stormy Pentland Firth from Thurso to Scapa Flow in the destroyer HMS *Oak*. He had never been a good sailor and was unwell during the crossing. He was received by Admiral Jellicoe and the flag officers of the British Grand Fleet, and listened at lunch with interest as they recounted their exploits in the Battle of Jutland, which had taken place only a few days earlier.

The *Hampshire* received her sailing orders on 4 June: to depart the following day for Archangel in northern Russia – a journey of 1,649 miles. She was to pass up the east side of Orkney on a route that was regularly swept for mines and to maintain a speed of not less than 18 knots up to Latitude 62°N. She was instructed to pass midway between the Shetlands and Orkney and keep not less than 200 miles from the Norwegian coast on her journey north. She would have a protective screen of two destroyer escorts as far north as Latitude 62°N, and from there on she would proceed alone at 16 knots, zigzagging to avoid torpedo attack.

On 5 June, however, the weather worsened and by the afternoon, a gale was blowing from the north-east. A heavy sea was running along the east coast, making minesweeping difficult. The Admiralty felt that the heavy sea would make it difficult for the *Hampshire*'s two destroyer escorts to keep up with the bigger and more powerful cruiser. So the plan was changed and it was decided to send *Hampshire* by one of the western routes. Of the two available routes there, it was decided to use the route set up in January 1916, which went past Hoy. This route was not regularly swept for mines but it was thought that no German minelayer would dare to operate this close to the heavily protected British base. This route would give the destroyers some shelter from the north-easterly gale and enable them to keep up with the *Hampshire*.

The fateful decision having been made, *Hampshire* slipped her mooring buoy and cleared the harbour at about 4.40 p.m. She steamed out of the Flow through Hoxa Sound to the south and then turned westwards into the stormy weather of the Pentland Firth, to rendezvous with her escort destroyers, *Victor* and *Unity*, off Tor Ness on the south-west of Hoy. The two destroyers fell into line behind *Hampshire*.

The prevailing weather conditions had however been misinterpreted, for within an hour, the storm centre had passed overhead and the wind backed sharply to the north-west. The conditions now facing *Hampshire* and her escorts were exactly the opposite of what had been predicted.

At 6.05 p.m., the smaller and less powerful destroyer *Victor*, signaled that she could only maintain 15 knots. At 6.10 p.m., *Unity* then signaled that she could only maintain 12 knots, and shortly afterwards at 6.18 p.m., signaled that she could only make ten knots. At 6.20 p.m., *Hampshire* signaled that *Unity* should return to base. Shortly after this, *Victor* signaled that she could not maintain any speed greater than 12 knots, and so at 6.30 p.m., *Hampshire* signaled that she should also return to base. The destroyers were off the entrance to Hoy Sound when they turned for home. *Hampshire* went on alone, fighting the fury of the force nine strong gale.

Hampshire struggled to make progress up the west coast against the gale for an hour. She dipped and crashed in the raging seas and the bow splash billowed over her fo'c'stle – she was only able to make 13.5 knots. At about 7.40.pm., when she was about 1.5 miles from shore between Marwick Head and the Brough of Birsay, a rumbling explosion suddenly shook the whole ship as she hit a mine. A hole was torn in her keel between her bows and the bridge, the helm jammed and the lights gradually went out as the power failed. With no power, she could not make radio contact with the shore to call for assistance.

The explosion seemed to have taken place on the port side, just forward of the bridge and according to survivors, it seemed to tear the heart right out of the ship. She immediately began to settle into the water and a cloud of brown, suffocating smoke poured up from the stokers' mess forward,

Above: Starboard side prop of the HMS Hampshire on display at Lyness Naval Museum.

Left: Port side prop HMS Hampshire © Ewan Rowell

making it difficult to see on the bridge. Most of the crew had been down below decks and most of the hatches were battened down and shored up for the night. The crew began to knock out the wedges and proceed to their stations. The after-hatch to the quarterdeck was open, and as the crew streamed aft away from the explosion, an officer was heard to call out: 'Make way for Lord Kitchener.' He passed by, clad in a greatcoat, and went up the after-hatch, just in front of one of the few survivors. He was last seen standing on the deck of the *Hampshire*, and it can only be assumed that he went down with the ship.

The cruiser settled quickly into the water by the bows. There was no power to work the lifeboat derricks and so none of the larger lifeboats could be hoisted out. Those smaller boats that were lowered into the water were smashed to pieces against the side of the *Hampshire* by the force of the gale. Not a single survivor saw any boat get clear away from the ship. A number of men took their places in the large lifeboats (which could not be lowered) in the forlorn hope that as the ship went down, these boats would float off. But these boats and crew were carried down with the *Hampshire* by the suction she created.

At about 7.50 p.m., only ten to 15 minutes after striking the mine, *Hampshire* went down bows first, heeling over to starboard with smoke and flame belching from just behind the bridge. Her stern lifted slowly out of the water and her propellers were seen clear of the water, still revolving as she went under.

Only three oval cork and wood Carley floats got away from the sinking ship. These rigid Carley floats were made from a length of copper tubing divided into waterproof sections, bent into an oval ring, then surrounded by cork or kapok and covered with a layer of waterproofed canvas. The raft was rigid and could remain buoyant even if the waterproof outer skin of individual compartments was punctured. One Carley float had only six men in it and faced with the severe conditions, it was flung over twice, jettisoning the men into the sea. Only two men were alive when it reached the safety of Skaill Bay.

A second larger Carley float got away with 40 to 50 men on it. When it made the shore just north of Skaill Bay five hours later at 1.15 a.m., only four of its occupants had survived the ordeal.

The third Carley float had about 40 men in it when it left the sinking ship and another 30 were picked up from the water. The men were drenched and badly affected by wind chill; most of them were soon suffering from exposure, losing consciousness or foaming slightly at the mouth. Those that lost consciousness never regained it. Almost five hours later, at 1 a.m., when it finally surged up on to the rocks in a small creek called Nebbi Geo, half a mile north of Skaill Bay, there were only six men left alive.

Iconic WWI recruiting poster featuring Lord Kitchener. He's pointing and looking at you no matter where you are.

54

The subsequent search at sea located 13 mines in the vicinity of the wreck site. These were laid at a depth of seven to nine metres – deep enough to let smaller vessels such as fishing boats or minesweepers sail over the top of them and designed to catch only the bigger vessels.

It was later revealed that a spread of 22 mines had been laid by *U-75* on 29 May as part of German plans for what had developed into the Battle of Jutland four days earlier. The German High Seas Fleet had put to sea to lure the British Battlecruiser Fleet out of its anchorage in the Firth of Forth. It was anticipated that the main British Grand Fleet based at Scapa Flow would also put to sea and German U-boats would be waiting for it. Three mine-laying U-boats, including *U-75*, were sent out to mine the likely areas the British Fleet would pass – and German intelligence was aware of the route that would tragically be used by the *Hampshire*. *U-75* sailed from Germany two days before Jellicoe even knew of Lord Kitchener's proposed journey.

With the death of Lord Kitchener, the Germans had unintentionally scored an immense victory that struck at the hearts of the British people. Kitchener may have been out of favour, but he was still a legend. The great liberator of the Sudan from Muslim aggression, he had led the relief force that had lifted the Mahdi's siege of Khartoum, in an attempt to save that other hero of the British Empire, General Gordon. He had quelled the Boer uprising in South Africa and on his return home had been given a rapturous and patriotic welcome. It was thus natural that at the outbreak of World War I, Britain should have turned to its supreme warlord for leadership and appointed him Secretary of State for War. His loss was an untimely and bitter blow for the nation.

Today, the wreck of HMS *Hampshire* lies in 70 metres of water at 59° 07.03 N and 03° 23.76 W, about 1.5 miles out from the sheer cliffs of Marwick Head. The Kitchener Memorial rises up very prominently from the nearest land point to the wreck: a solemn reminder that brings home very movingly the tragedy that struck all those years ago. This wreck is a very sensitive war grave of particular interest to the Ministry of Defence and to the people of Orkney – and in 2002 was classified as a controlled site under The Protection of Military Remains Act 1986. Accordingly no diving is now permitted on this wreck unless licensed by the Ministry of Defence.

HMS *Hampshire* was a sizeable and powerful Devonshire class, first-class armoured cruiser of 10,850 tons displacement. She measured 475 feet in length, with a beam of 68 ft 6 in. and a draft of 24 feet. Powered by a two-shaft, four-cylinder engine that was fed by six boilers aft and 17 Yarrow water-tube boilers (distributed between the three forward boiler rooms) she could make 22 knots.

HMS *Hampshire* was a potent fighting ship carrying four 7.5-inch guns, six 6-inch guns, two 12-pounders, eighteen 3-pounders and two 18-inch torpedo tubes. Her main armour belt ranged from 2 to 6 inches thick, her armoured bulkheads were 5 inches thick, her turrets 5 inches and her barbettes 6 inches. Her decks had ¾ to 2 inches of armour against plunging fire. She carried a ship's complement of 655 men.

The Devonshire class vessels were provided under the 1901–02 Programme, in an attempt to improve on the Monmouth design without an excessive increase in size. Both armour and armament were improved with single 7.5-inch gun-turrets added in place of the previous two twin 6-inch gun-turrets. While under construction, however, two more single 7.5-inch turrets were mounted abreast the foremast. The main armour belt was increased to a six-inch thickness and reduced in height by a foot. The class was contemporary with the King Edward VII class battleships.

HMS *Hampshire* was built at the Chatham Dockyard, being laid down on 25 March 1902, launched on 30 April 1904 and completed on 24 August 1905 when she joined the 1st Cruiser Squadron of the Channel Fleet. She was refitted at Portsmouth in 1908 and recommissioned in the 3rd Division Home Fleet in August 1909. In December 1911, she joined the 6th Cruiser Squadron, Mediterranean Fleet.

Hampshire was sent to China in 1912, where she served until the outbreak of World War I. She captured a German merchantman on 11 August 1914 and took part in the famous hunt for the German light cruiser

Emden, which Vice-Admiral Maximilian Graf von Spee, in charge of the East Asia Squadron, had dispatched to the Indian Ocean on detachment on 13 August 1914 to harass Allied shipping. Ingeniously, the *Emden's* captain, Commander Karl von Müller, added a false fourth funnel en route as he passed through the neutral Dutch East Indies to make *Emden* look like a British light cruiser. *Emden* sighted the immensely more powerful *Hampshire* off Sumatra, but managed to elude her and went on to sink a succession of Allied vessels, before being engaged and sunk by the Australian light cruiser *Sydney* on 9 November near the British Cocos Islands.

HMS *Hampshire* subsequently joined the British Grand Fleet in December 1914, becoming part of the 7th Cruiser Squadron in January 1915. She was sent to the White Sea to protect shipping in November 1915 and then, serving with the 2nd Cruiser Squadron, took part in the Battle of Jutland on 31 May 1916. She subsequently made her way to Scapa Flow for her fateful departure to Russia with Lord Kitchener on 5 June 1916.

The wreck of HMS *Hampshire* today lies almost completely upside down with only a slight list – her starboard side has sunk right into the seabed and her port side is raised slightly higher.

HMS *Hampshire* had two massive 43-ton phosphor bronze three-bladed propellers: one mounted either side of the central keel strip, with a free section of shaft running out some way from the keel and being locked in place just forward of the propeller itself by a substantial A-frame bracket. Only the portside propeller remains on the wreck. The starboard propeller and part of its free section of shaft and wood-lined tunnel were removed without permission in 1983. There was considerable public outcry at this and as the salvage vessel called into Peterhead Harbour the propeller was offloaded onto the pier – where it lay for many years. Eventually it was returned to Orkney where it is now on display at the entrance to the Lyness Naval Museum on Hoy.

Underneath the upturned hull at the stern, part of the after 7.5-inch gun-turret can be made out – its barrel resting on the seabed. The rudder has fallen to lie flat on the seabed nearby.

The hull of HMS *Hampshire* has rotted through in places and is now losing its structural integrity. A row of portholes, most still intact, runs along the complete length of the hull and above this row, for most of the length of the hull on the port side is an intermittent tear or fissure where the weight of the upturned hull is pressing down. This tear is at the bottom of the structurally strong armour belt where the weaker unarmoured hull bottom meets it. The hull will eventually collapse and fall in here. Sections of the mainmast lie on the seabed, still with large shackles on them for fixed rigging. Two prominent bilge keels run along most of the length of the upturned hull.

Nearer the bow, the outline of the port side 7.5-inch gun-turret, which was mounted abreast of the foremast, can be made out – although it is almost entirely covered by plating from past salvage operations. The bow itself has been removed, partly by the original mine explosion and partly by the attentions of salvers – right down to the underside of the upturned main deck. This has produced a debris field within the confines of the hull. In the midst of the debris, the cylindrical barbette from the forward single 7.5-inch gun-turret lies fallen on its side.

Shipwreck – the essentials	
Type of wreck	Devonshire first class armoured cruiser
Nationality	British
Year of construction	1902–5
Dimensions	475. x 68 ft 6 in. x 24 ft
Displacement (tons)	10,850
Date sunk	5 June 1916
Cause of sinking	mine
Depth of water	68 metres
Least depth above wreck	55 metres
Position	59° 07.03N, 003° 23.76W

The armoured cruiser HMS Hampshire.

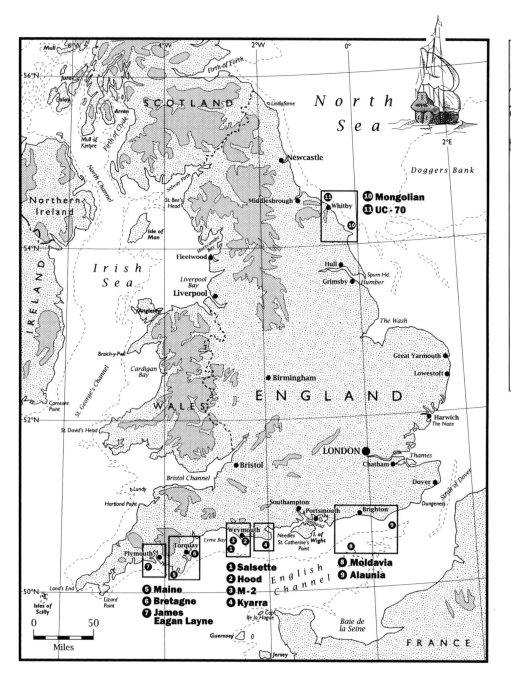

① **Salsette**
② **Hood**
③ **M-2**
④ **Kyarra**

⑤ **Maine**
⑥ **Bretagne**
⑦ **James
Eagan Layne**

⑧ **Moldavia**
⑨ **Alaunia**

⑩ **Mongolian**
⑪ **UC - 70**

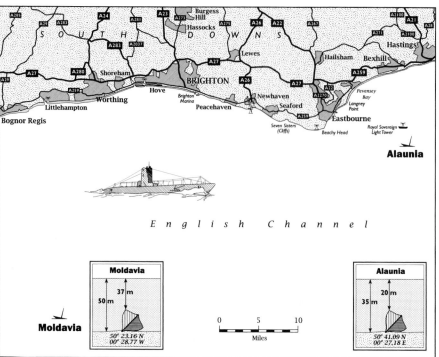

Moldavia

50 m
37 m

*50° 23.16 N
00° 28.77 W*

Moldavia

Alaunia

35 m
20 m

*50° 41.09 N
00° 27.18 E*

Alaunia

Above: Location chart for Moldavia *and* Alaunia I.

Left: Location chart for English shipwrecks.

2

ENGLISH CHANNEL

THE P&O PASSENGER LINER *MOLDAVIA*, LITTLEHAMPTON, WEST SUSSEX

The P&O liner *Moldavia* was built on the Clyde in 1903 by J. Caird and Co., Greenock. She was 520 ft 6 in. long with a beam of 58 ft 3 in., and powered by two triple-expansion engines, she could reach speeds of 18.5 knots – fast for her day. She is perhaps one of the most revered and well-loved wrecks in the English Channel, lying 26 miles out in about 50 metres of water. The wreck itself is vast, hauntingly beautiful and still full of items of interest. Portholes hang open, their brass and glass fitments still in place. The massive anchors are still held snugly in their hawse pipes, despite the ravages of more than 90 years at the bottom of the Channel. The sea life is immense and large schools of fish drift over the wreck, sometimes hanging like a curtain obscuring the ship itself.

In her heyday, her two large raked-back funnels were set at the same angle as her stylish foremast and mainmast to give her a sleek, modern look. The

The haunting remains of the P&O liner Moldavia.

The P&O liner Moldavia.

The Moldavia *arriving at Fremantle, near Perth, Australia.*

main central superstructure housed the bridge, captain's accommodation and saloons at the front and extended back for almost half the length of the vessel, rising up for two deck levels. Wooden lifeboats hung on davits either side atop. In addition to a substantial cargo-carrying ability, she carried 348 first-class passengers and 166 second-class. *Moldavia* was a very famous ship in her pre-war days – well known on the Britain to Australia run.

Two years into World War I, in 1915, the British Government requisitioned her for war service. She was fitted out with 4.7-inch guns and became the armed merchant cruiser HMS *Moldavia* – joining the 10th Cruiser Squadron to enforce the blockade between the north of Scotland and Iceland. The Squadron was based in the Shetland Islands and its duties included the interception of merchant ships. Armed guards would go onboard to ensure the ship sailed to an allied port for its cargo to be inspected. Her gunners sank the abandoned ship SS *Patio* in November 1916. Her 4.7-inch guns were latterly removed and eight more powerful 6-inch guns were fitted. In February 1917 she intercepted the Italian ship SS *Famiglia*, which had already been intercepted by a German U-boat, which had put an armed guard aboard and ordered her to sail to Germany. The Germans set off scuttling charges and she was abandoned. *Moldavia* thereafter served as a convoy escort between West Africa and Plymouth.

Following the Battle of Jutland in 1916, when it became clear that the German Navy had been deterred from any further fleet action against the Royal Navy, auxiliary cruisers such as *Moldavia* were no longer required and due to her great speed and size she was turned over for use as a troopship. In 1918, she was sent to America to collect troops for the European battlefields who were completing their training at Camp Mills, New York.

On 11 May, the 907 men of the 58th Regiment of the US 8th Infantry Brigade boarded the dazzle-painted *Moldavia* bound for Europe. The slow crossing of the Atlantic was completed successfully and on the night of 23 May 1918, now in a convoy of five large steamships protected by Royal Navy destroyers, she started up the English Channel en route for France. A strict blackout was in force on the ships – every porthole was blacked out and no light was permitted that might reveal the convoy to the enemy. All aboard knew they were now entering the most dangerous part of their voyage: the U-boat killing ground.

The evening before, *UB-57* of the Flanders Flotilla, had left Zeebruge and successfully passed through the Belgian coastal barrage: a wall of steel nets with mines suspended at different heights. *UB-57* then passed through the Dover nets and entered the Dover Straits. Here, between Folkestone and Cap Gris Nez, was another wall of nets and mines, which were linked to sound detector loops. These loops enabled mines to be set off remotely from the shore if an unidentified vessel was detected passing by. On the surface, fast Royal Navy sub-hunters patrolled as giant searchlights swept across the seas.

UB-57 successfully penetrated all these British defences and then took up a position on the surface, near the Owers Lightship – which both the Allied and German U-boats used for navigation fixing. It was common for Allied merchant vessels to pass close to it. In the welcoming cover of darkness, *UB-57*'s engines were switched off and the U-boat rocked gently on the surface, whilst high in the conning tower, spotters scanned the horizon with binoculars. The convoy was sighted.

Shipwreck – the essentials

Type of wreck	P&O cargo/passenger liner
Nationality	British
Launched	1903
Dimensions	520.6 ft x 58.3 ft
Tonnage	9,500 grt
Date sunk	23 May 1918
Cause of sinking	torpedoed by *UB-57*
Depth of water	50 metres
Least depth above wreck	37 metres
Position	50° 23.16N, 000° 28.768W

Immediately, *UB-57*'s engines were restarted and she set off on the surface in pursuit. Gradually the gap closed on the slower convoy and soon *UB-57* was in a firing position. She submerged to await her prey, hidden by the sea. As *UB-57*'s commander watched through the periscope, the convoy, which was zigzagging to avoid torpedo attack, made a turn and the lead ship, the *Moldavia*, started to head directly towards *UB-57*.

A bow torpedo was fired and exploded on *Moldavia*'s port side amidships. The explosion was heard and felt all over the ship and 56 American troops in an adjacent compartment were killed instantly. Fifteen minutes after the explosion, *Moldavia* slewed to a wallowing halt. As escorting Royal Navy destroyers started a depth-charge pattern at the scene of the attack, onboard damage reports made it clear that the ship was doomed.

Moldavia started to settle by the head. Her majestic bows disappeared first beneath the water, their water-filled weight dragging the front of the ship under and forcing her great stern to lift upwards. Her massive twin screws and rudder rose up and held there for a moment, seemingly suspended and motionless before she started her final plunge down through 150 feet of water to the bottom.

Today, the wreck of the *Moldavia* lies 26 miles out into the English Channel on her port side – hiding the damage from the torpedo strike. Her majestic bow still shows its beautiful straight stem, and on deck nearby are situated her massive anchor winches and a tripod crane for lifting and fitting a spare anchor. Her foredeck cargo hatches are now open and her large midships superstructure – the most prominent feature of the wreck – has collapsed to the seabed: a jumble of interesting pieces of ship. The hull itself is collapsing now, but is still lined with portholes – some with their brass and glass fitments still in place.

Although she rests in 50 metres of water, the uppermost side of the wreck is reached at 37 metres and with the general good visibility this far out into the Channel, as you swim above the ship it is usually possible to see all the way down to the seabed

© Rod Macdonald

Above right: RMS Alaunia I. Courtesy Merseyside Views

Above: The wreck of the liner RMS Alaunia I.

THE CUNARD LINER RMS *ALAUNIA I*, HASTINGS, EAST SUSSEX

The massive 13,495-grt Cunard liner *Alaunia I* is the largest diveable wreck off the East Sussex coast. Although she has been commercially salvaged, the wreck remains a tantalising glimpse of a once-majestic ocean-going liner, vast in scale.

Alaunia I was built in 1913 in the run-up to World War I. The Cunard Line had inaugurated its own Canadian service in 1911 and the company needed its own fast purpose-built ships for that profitable route. Three vessels for the route were ordered from Scotts Shipbuilding & Engineering Co. of Greenock, Glasgow: the *Andania*, *Alaunia I* and the *Aurania*. *Alaunia I* was the second of these three ships to be launched – on 9 June 1913. She was 540 ft long with a beam of 64 ft and accommodation for 520 second-class and 1,620 third-class passengers. The usual third-class dormitories of other liners were replaced in this vessel by four- and six-berth cabins.

Like her two sister ships, *Alaunia I* was fitted with two masts, and had two towering funnels amidships in the Cunard Line's classic red colour with black bands at the top.

Alaunia I's maiden voyage on 27 November 1913 was a passage from Liverpool to Boston via Queenstown and Portland. She arrived in Boston on 6 December 1913. She then went on to make continuous regular Atlantic crossings throughout the first half of 1914, taking emigrants to new lives in America.

In August 1914, as arrangements were being made to transport the First Contingent of the Canadian Expeditionary Force to the battlefields of Europe, the British Government requisitioned her for use as a troopship. More than 30 ships were required to transport 30,000 officers and men, 7,679 horses, 70 field guns, 110 motor vehicles and 705 horse-drawn vehicles across the north Atlantic. Canada, at that time an unmilitary nation, had raised this large force in just six weeks following the outbreak of war. The massive *Alaunia I* was perfect for the task.

A powerful Royal Navy force was assembled to escort and protect the armada during its Atlantic crossing. Four cruisers, the pre-dreadnought battleship HMS *Glory*, the Lion class battlecruiser HMS *Princess Royal* and the Majestic class pre-dreadnought HMS *Magnificent* were assigned to rendezvous with the convoy. A second battleship from Britain would rendezvous with the group during the passage across the Atlantic.

Admiral Jellicoe, in charge of the British Grand Fleet at Scapa Flow, made careful and detailed preparations on the British side of the Atlantic to try to ensure the safe passage of the vital convoy. On 3 October 1914, the British Grand Fleet deployed from Scapa Flow and took up strategic positions to ensure that no German warships broke out from the North Sea during the vital week when the convoy approached Britain. The precautions worked – the convoy with its precious cargo of men and machines arrived safely.

The *Alaunia* was subsequently involved in supporting the Gallipoli landings of 1915. When the Allies withdrew from Gallipoli in 1916, having suffered some 250,000 casualties but without having gained any ground, *Alaunia* went back to carrying troops to the European theatre from Canada and America.

On 19 September 1916, she left London on a return voyage to New York. On 19 October, having safely re-crossed the Atlantic on the return leg of her voyage, as she headed up the English Channel for London, when she was two miles south of the Royal Sovereign Lightship, off Eastbourne, East Sussex she was suddenly rocked without warning by an enormous explosion. She had struck a mine. An alert was put out and as rescue vessels headed towards her, she started to settle slowly into the water.

An initial attempt was made to take the ship in tow with tugs and run for shore to beach her. The damage caused by the mine however was too severe – and when it became clear that she was going to founder before the shallows could be reached, the order was given for the ship to be abandoned. All passengers and 163 of the crew were safely taken ashore. Two of the crew sadly perished.

Today, the wreck of the *Alaunia* lies several miles south of Eastbourne in 35 metres of water. She wreck sits on her keel, although the bow has broken off and rolled over onto its port side. The ship has been extensively worked by commercial salvers, however she retains her ship shape and has much of interest for the diver to see – from massive steering gear at the stern to her boilers and propeller shaft.

Shipwreck – the essentials	
Type of wreck	Cunard liner
Nationality	British
Launched	9 June 1913
Dimensions	540.0 ft x 64 ft
Tonnage	13,405 grt
Date sunk	19 October 1916
Cause of sinking	mine
Depth of water	35 metres
Least depth above wreck	20 metres
Position	50° 41.09N, 000° 27.18W

THE P&O LINER *SALSETTE*, LYME BAY, DORSET

The 5,842-ton P&O express mail liner *Salsette* was regarded in the period before World War I as one of the most beautiful straight-stemmed steamships ever built. A sleek, elegant ocean-going liner, her hull was a uniform brilliant white, studded by two layers of some 600 portholes running her complete length. Her mainmast and foremast were set at a rakish angle, matching her two yellow funnels. She summed up the look of class and opulence that marked fine sea-going vessels of the era. Yet for all her elegance and speed, the dark clouds and grim deeds of World War I would overtake her and consign her to the depths of the English Channel for eternity, when towards the end of the war in 1917, she was attacked and

The haunting remains of the P&O liner Salsette *in Lyme Bay.*

torpedoed by *UB-40*. Fatally wounded, she sank into 44 metres of cold dark water – yet another testament to man's inhumanity to man.

The *Salsette* was built in 1908 for the express mail service of the Peninsular and Oriental Steam Navigation Co. – the famous P&O – by J. Caird and Co. in Greenock, Scotland. She was 440 ft long with a beam of 53 ft 2 in. and a draft of 19 ft 6 in. She was a fast ship, built for the long passage to India – her namesake is a small island off Bombay. After her completion, in the summer of 1908, during sea trials she managed 19.5 knots. Although her hull was painted white, her superstructure was initially painted the P&O standard light-stone colour, but this soon gave way to white overall with yellow funnels: she cut a dashing figure.

In October 1908, she set out on her first working voyage to Bombay, and despite being held up for several hours in the Suez Canal, she was able to break the company's Marseilles to Bombay record. She also went on to break the longstanding Bombay to Aden record with a time of 3 days, 19 hours and 7 minutes. This entitled her to fly the golden cockerel emblem of the P&O on her jack staff: the signal that she was the fastest vessel in the P&O fleet. She would later go on to win the Blue Riband for the fastest crossing of the Atlantic.

In 1915, as the stalemate of trench warfare consumed the lives of the combatants in vast numbers, because the Admiralty had already requisitioned many of the regular mail ships, the *Salsette* was ordered back to Britain, put on the London to Bombay mail service, and then on the service to Australia. By that time, although the U-boat threat was fully appreciated, it was thought that the liner's great speed of 20 knots would make her able to outrun any enemy U-boat. The fastest U-boats could achieve speeds of only around 7 knots underwater and about 13 knots if running on the surface. However, in July 1917, sheer bad luck brought her close to a 260-ton U-boat, *UB-40*.

UB-40 was a small and slow U-boat, part of the Flanders Flotilla based in Zeebruge and Bruges. She could only manage 9 knots on the surface

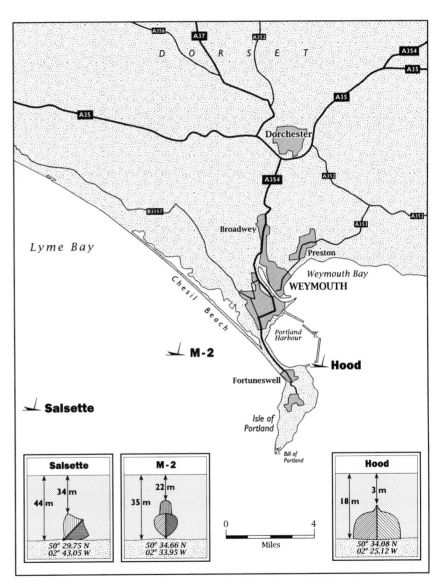

Location chart for Salsette, HMS/M *M2 &* HMS Hood.

The 5,842-ton P&O express mail liner Salsette.

Howaldt quickly submerged *UB-40* to periscope-depth, put the boat's engines ahead and headed towards the oncoming vessels – one of which was the *Salsette*.

Under the command of Captain A. B. Armitage, RNR, the *Salsette* had anchored at 7 p.m. in the Downs, off the east Kent coast the evening before: 19 July. At 10.30 p.m., Captain Armitage received his sailing orders to proceed to Bombay. As the *Salsette* started off on her long journey, she approached the Shambles Lightship. Here, a patrol vessel signalled the course she was to take. The *Salsette* started to work up speed and commenced zigzagging, following her Admiralty instructions. She had moved down the Channel as far as Lyme Bay, moving at speed and zigzagging, when on one of these turns she passed right across the firing position that Howaldt had taken up.

At just after 12.01 p.m., Howaldt gave the order to fire from close range. The *Salsette*'s chief officer, who was on the monkey-bridge taking bearings, spotted the torpedo track and shouted out: "Hard a-starboard".

Captain Armitage, on hearing the commotion, rushed out from the chart room, but the ship had been given no time to avoid the torpedo. There was a huge explosion on her starboard side that threw Captain Armitage to the ground. A column of water – the classic sign of a torpedo strike – exploded upwards to hang suspended in the air. Fourteen Indian firemen (employed in the boiler room to feed coal to the boilers) died immediately, as the hull of the ship was torn open.

Despite all her watertight doors being shut and her main deck scuttles being fitted with deadlights that prevented water getting into the ship, the damage to her hull was so catastrophic that nothing could prevent her flooding. She was doomed.

Within five minutes of the strike, the lifeboats had been filled, lowered and were pulling away from the mortally stricken ship. Captain Armitage and a few officers stayed behind along with Lifeboat No. 3, to ensure that no secret or militarily sensitive documents and papers were left aboard. The ship might have remained afloat long enough to be boarded and searched by the U-boat crew. The ship's papers were placed in a weighted bag and thrown over the side. Captain Armitage ordered the radio operator to

and 5–6 knots submerged. She was not able to chase her prey: she had to wait until it fell into her path.

UB-40 was commanded by Oberleutnant zur See Howaldt, one of Germany's ace submariners and one of the few who would survive the war – when the average life span of a U-boat captain was just 60 days.

In the middle of July 1917, Howaldt took *UB-40* from its base and slipped through the British barrage of nets and mines in the Channel. On 15 July he surfaced off the Sussex coast and sank a small group of English fishing boats with boarding-parties – a practice he also employed when dealing with sailing vessels, to save expending a valuable torpedo on small low-value vessels. After allowing the crew to abandon ship, he would use the deck gun or a bomb placed inside the ship below the waterline to sink the vessel.

From Sussex, *UB-40* proceeded to Lyme Bay, where, not seeing any targets, Howaldt prepared to wait until shipping came his way. It turned out to be a wait of four long days before, on 20 July, the tell-tale black smoke of the coal-fired engines of a big ship approaching from the east got the crew to action stations.

continuously send a message that *Salsette* was under submarine attack. This he did, until he was forced by the rising sea to leave the radio room for his own safety. Captain Armitage and his remaining crew boarded Lifeboat No. 3 and pulled away from the ship. Within 28 minutes of the torpedo strike, the *Salsette* had sunk from sight.

Royal Navy destroyers, alerted by the emergency sub-attack broadcast, arrived on the scene and started a pattern of depth charging. Huge crumping explosions reverberated through the depths, followed by secondary brilliant white eruptions of seawater. The destroyers searched extensively for the U-boat, forcing Howaldt to take her down to the seabed in the hope that his pursuers would pass by. After lying silently on the bottom for an hour and hearing the sounds of the British activity fading into the distance, Howaldt judged that all was clear and came up to periscope-depth.

Peering through the periscope, Howaldt could make out the British destroyers in the distance, continuing their depth-charging patterns. As he scanned the horizon, he saw a small steamship, the *L. H. Carl*: a 1,916-ton British steamship en route from Barry to Rouen, approaching his position. A lesser man, having just survived intense British depth charging may have let this vessel pass by and made good his escape. However, Howaldt was a tenacious captain and he immediately ordered his crew to prepare to attack the *L. H. Carl*. Howaldt again fired with great accuracy – his torpedo struck the *L. H. Carl*, fatally wounding her and sending her to the bottom very quickly, with the loss of two members of crew.

This further attack alerted the British destroyers to *UB-40*'s whereabouts. They charged over to the scene and started depth charging afresh. Skilfully, Howaldt was able to evade these attempts and head back for Zeebruge, which he would reach five days later, on 25 July.

Today the wreck of the once beautiful *Salsette* is justly acclaimed as one of the finest wrecks in English waters. She lies on her port side in 44 metres of water some 11.5 nautical miles west of Portland Bill with a least depth to her uppermost starboard rail of 34 metres. Although her superstructure has long since rotted away, the hull retains its fine shape and still shows off her classic straight stem bow. A tidal scour around the bow has excavated the seabed down to 46 metres.

Her majestic bow still shows off the classic straight stem. Nearby, both anchors are still snugly held in their hawses – their chains leading up through the hawse pipes and back along the deck to the anchor winches. Between the chains stands a small crane used for manoeuvring the anchors and shackling up and deploying the spare anchor. Two lines of portholes dot along either side of the hull. Both masts have broken and fallen to the seabed and cargo cranes and derricks are strewn around beside the hatches to her forward cargo holds. The midships' superstructure and her lightweight funnels have all collapsed to the seabed.

The torpedo from *UB-40* struck *Salsette* on the starboard side of the engine room and on the uppermost starboard side of the wreck the large hole left by the explosion is easily visible. At the very stern of the ship the uppermost starboard side propeller has been salvaged, Her 4.7-inch defensive gun still remains in situ.

Shipwreck – the essentials	
Type of wreck	P&O express mail liner
Nationality	British
Launched	1908
Dimensions	440 ft x 53.2 ft x 19.6 ft
Tonnage	5,842-grt
Date sunk	20 July 1917
Cause of sinking	torpedo from *UB-40*
Depth of water	44 metres
Least depth above wreck	34 metres
Position	50° 29.748N, 002° 43.049W

The atmospheric wreck of the submarine HMS/M M2 in Lyme Bay.

© Rod Macdonald

thick black plume of smoke from their coal-fired furnaces. However, the M class submarines with their lethal 12-inch battleship gun would be able to approach a target submerged and unseen, stealthily getting into a firing position that traditional surface vessels could not achieve. The submarine could then leave the scene of the attack submerged and undetected. A submarine that could approach an enemy unseen and fire from a partially submerged position – with only the top of the barrel and its bead sight projecting above the water – was certainly a revolutionary and potentially devastating idea. The drawback however was that only one shot could be fired from the part submerged position, as the sub had to surface to reload.

M2 displaced 1,594 tons surfaced and 1,946 tons submerged. She was a large submarine, some 90.1 metres in length, with a beam of 7.5 metres and a draft of 4.9 metres. She was fitted out with two Vickers 12-cylinder diesel engines for travel on the surface and two electric motors for running submerged. On the surface, her twin propellers could push her to speeds of 15 knots: submerged she could achieve 9 knots. Her maximum diving depth was 75 metres. She carried eight 18-inch torpedoes for her four bow tubes and was fitted with a 3-inch anti-aircraft gun mounted aft of her conning tower. Although her hull was laid down in 1916, her construction was not completed until 1920, after the war had ended.

Her 12-inch gun was removed in 1927 and in its place, in another radical piece of lateral thinking, a watertight hangar for a Parnell Peto – one of the smallest seaplanes in the world at the time – was fitted in front of the conning tower. This seaplane had wings that folded back to allow it to be stowed away in the hangar. The seaplane was launched by steam catapult from the foredeck and its role was to serve as a stealth reconnaissance aircraft that could appear without warning at locations outwith normal air-cover range, spot a foe or target, communicate the sighting and then, as if by magic, disappear beneath the waves again. The Peto on its return would land in the sea near the submarine and was then hoisted aboard by crane and re-stowed in its hanger.

On 26 January 1932, *M2* left Portland Harbour on exercise just after 9 a.m., in calm conditions but with a little fog about. She was initially to

Above: The Parnell Peto, wings extended, is readied for flight.

Right: The British submarine HMS/M M2 launching the world's smallest seaplane, a Parnell Peto.

THE SUBMARINE HMS/M *M2*, LYME BAY, DORSET

HMS/M *M2* is a 296-ft British submarine, one of the four M class submarines laid down in 1916 (replacing the order for the last four K class submarines K17-K21) during the dark days of World War I. She lies in easily accessible and relatively shallow waters not far offshore and is a rare glimpse of a hugely innovative and far-sighted development in submarine warfare, at a time when the full potential of the submarine as a weapon of war was being developed.

What made the M class so radically different was that for the first time, the Royal Navy would mount a powerful 12-inch battleship gun on the submarine's foredeck. Until then the largest gun on a submarine was 5-inch. Battleships until then had always given away their approach by the tell-tale

exercise alone in West Bay before rendezvousing with two other submarines for a combined exercise.

Just after 10 a.m., the commander of *M2* signalled to the command vessel that he was going to dive *M2*. Some hours later the busy wireless operators on the command vessel, swamped by messages from the exercise, realised that there had been no further communication from the submarine. *M2* then failed to return to Portland Harbour at her scheduled time of 4.15 p.m. A search was then initiated, but by 8 p.m., no trace of her had been found and a full-scale emergency was declared. Ratings ashore were recalled to their ships to start a search. Theatre and cinema shows were halted and managers went onstage to make the recall announcements. By 9 p.m., some 500 men had returned to their ships.

The authorities knew that if *M2* had sunk, she could be sitting incapacitated on the seabed with her crew still alive. Her air supplies would start to dwindle, but she carried sufficient for her crew to survive for another 48 hours submerged.

Just after midnight, the Admiralty announced that an object presumed to be *M2* had been found three miles west of Portland Bill in 17 fathoms. Submarine salvage ships rushed to the scene and divers attempted to descend down to the contact - but heavy tides and difficult seas made it impossible for them to reach it. They got down to a depth of 70 feet, some 30 feet short of the bottom, before having to ascend.

By the afternoon of the following day, 27 January, the mood of the rescuers was turning gloomy. Telegrams were sent to the families of the crew; their stark, bare lines striking fear into those who received them: 'Regret to inform you that your husband is missing and feared drowned in submarine *M2*, believed sunk off Portland on Tuesday.'

At 10.30 p.m, that night the Admiralty issued a statement confirming that the divers' further attempts to reach the contact had failed due to the conditions, but that diving would continue throughout the night where possible.

The Royal Navy continued trying to identify and dive targets in West Bay – which was ominously known as the Bay of a Thousand Wrecks. It was a colossal task, using the location methods of the time: a simple wire sweep to snag underwater obstructions. The following day however, 28 January, the captain of another ship reported to the Admiralty that he had seen a submarine with an 'M' mark on her conning tower diving rapidly in a completely different location, and unusually, going down stern first.

Shipwreck – the essentials	
Type of wreck	submarine
Nationality	British
Launched	1920
Dimensions	296ft x 24ft 8"
Tonnage	1,594 surfaced, 1,946 submerged
Date sunk	26 January 1932
Cause of sinking	flooding during exercise
Depth of water	35 metres
Least depth above wreck	22 metres
Position	50° 34.55N, 002° 33.95W

At 5 a.m. on 29 January, the Admiralty announced that divers had successfully made it down to the first contact but found it to be an old wreck. Later that evening, the Admiralty made a further announcement that all the obstructions examined by divers had proved to be old wrecks but that the search would continue. For the following five days, the continuous regime of laboriously searching for a contact and then sending divers down to check, failed to reveal the resting place of *M2*. Each time divers went down, they reported an old wreck.

On 2 February, newspapers ran a story of a fisherman who had reported picking up the body of a man in a white submarine-issue sweater in West Bay. The body had fallen back into the sea whilst attempts were being made to retrieve it and had been lost. The same day, the Admiralty reported that

The pre-dreadnought battleship HMS Hood.

the hatch from the hanger, down into the sub.

Today, the wreck of HMS/M *M2* sits upright on a sandy seabed in 35 metres of water. At her bow, either side of her straight stem can be located her four 18-inch torpedo tubes just forward of her diving planes. A small anchor is still held snug in its hawse. The 8-ft high seaplane hanger on her foredeck is open and now part filled with silt. On the foredeck just in front of it the Carey compressed air catapult for launching her seaplane is still in place – the seaplane floats fitted on either side of the ramp.

Above the hanger door sits the crane for recovering the seaplane – its rotating boom now part sheared off. Behind the hanger stands the conning tower, which rises up to 22 metres and still has its periscopes in place.

The open conning tower navigating bridge sweeps back to the rear, before the sheer drop to the 3-inch AA gun platform – the gun itself now missing. At her seemingly delicate stern her rudder is still in place - flanked either side by the free section of her prop shafts and diving planes.

M2 is a big submarine – at almost 300 feet long she is larger than many steamships of the time. She is a fascinating glimpse of a historic branch of submarine evolution.

THE BATTLESHIP HMS *HOOD*, PORTLAND HARBOUR, DORSET

The British pre-dreadnought battleship HMS *Hood* was commissioned in 1889, and was the eighth battleship provided for by the Naval Defence Act of March 1889. At the time of her launch at Chatham two years later in 1891, she was a state-of-the-art vehicle of war, heavily armed and heavily armoured. She symbolised the power and might of the Royal Navy and

the Navy had retrieved a cap belonging to the coxswain of *M2*, floating in a canvas bag; and then on a sweep wire, a collar belonging to a chief petty officer was found.

On 3 February, the Admiralty finally announced that *M2* had been found and positively identified by divers who reported that the seaplane hangar door and the upper conning tower hatch were open.

Over the coming months there were various attempts made to raise *M2* to the surface – but all failed. On one occasion, the body of a pilot in full flying kit was found about 15 feet away from the submarine and it was assumed that he had been getting ready to man the plane when the sub sunk.

The subsequent Admiralty enquiry concluded that *M2* had foundered as she surfaced and prepared to launch her seaplane. The main hanger door had been opened – perhaps too early – and water flooded her hull through

© Rod Macdonald

The upturned wreck of HMS Hood *still lies as a blockship between the two southern piers of Portland Harbour (inset).*

boasted to the world of the prowess of the nation that created her.

At the time of her launch, she was seen as a colossal and powerful fighting machine, displacing 14,150 tons and 15,588 tons at combat load. She was 410 ft in length with a beam of 75 ft and a draft of 27.5 ft. *Hood* was fitted with four 13.5-inch guns in two twin turrets as her main armament, and a secondary armament mainly consisting of ten independently-fired, quick firing 6-inch guns, set in single turrets ranged along either side of the ship.

Hood was protected by an 18-inch-thick main armour belt with 4 inches of hard-faced steel above as protection against secondary weapons. Her deck armour was 3 inches thick and her barbettes (the armoured cylinders that descended from her main gun-turrets to the magazines below) had walls 17 inches thick.

Following her launch, HMS *Hood* quickly gained a reputation as a good-looking battleship, but a very poor seagoing vessel. She had a forward freeboard of only 11ft 3 inches compared to the 20 feet of the other ships of her class. She was weighed down greatly by her old fashioned, 19th century, 13.5-inch armoured gun-turrets, which had a cumbersome rotating mount. These heavy turrets added to the amount of weight high up on the ship (compared to later barbettes within the hull) and lowered her freeboard. She needed very calm conditions if she were to make any decent speed. In heavier seas, her bow dipped and burrowed into the waves, resulting in a lot of water and spray sweeping the ship and making effective gunnery difficult. She was ill suited to the North Sea and Atlantic waters, and so not long after her completion, she was sent to the quieter waters of the Mediterranean.

Just 15 years after her launch, the construction in 1906 of HMS *Dreadnought* completely revolutionised warship design. She was such a quantum leap forward in battleship design, that overnight she rendered all the warships that had gone before her obsolete – and gave her name to the new breed of battleships: 'dreadnoughts'. Earlier battleships such as HMS *Hood* suddenly became obsolete 'pre-dreadnoughts' – and by the advent of World War I, HMS *Hood* was deemed unfit to fight.

The new dreadnoughts were about 10 per cent bigger than their predecessor pre-dreadnoughts. They were faster, had thicker armour and greater firepower. Each had ten 12-inch guns set in five twin turrets, compared to *Hood*'s four 13.5-inch guns in two twin turrets. The first dreadnought guns were able to hurl 850 lb shells for 18,500 yards – and the distance soon increased as new classes of dreadnoughts were built. *Hood* had a range of less than 16,000 yards.

The new dreadnoughts could fire a broadside of eight shells from their main guns to either side, whilst the pre-dreadnoughts such as HMS *Hood* fired a broadside of just four shells. The dreadnoughts could also fire six shells ahead, whilst the pre-dreadnoughts could only fire two. But an increase in firepower and protective armour was only half the story. In yet another quantum leap in battleship design, for the first time ever, all eight guns in a broadside (which on pre-dreadnoughts were fired independently) could now be aimed and fired in unison by just one gunnery officer. One dreadnought could match two pre-dreadnoughts for firepower at long range, and three pre-dreadnoughts when firing ahead.

Hood and her sister Royal Sovereign R class battleships had a maximum speed of 17.5 knots, whereas the new dreadnoughts could achieve a much faster speed of 23 knots. Thus *Hood* and her pre-dreadnought sister ships were doomed to become slow, obsolete ships, unable to keep up with the main fleet.

During the years from 1905 to 1910, coinciding with the development and deployment of HMS *Dreadnought* and her class of superior battleships, the Royal Sovereign R Class battleships such as *Hood* were taken out of the frontline fleet and put on reserve duties. She was later transferred to Portland as a target for torpedo practice and her heavy guns were taken out.

With the outbreak of World War I, most of the Royal Sovereign R Class battleships were sent for scrapping or used as gunnery targets. HMS *Hood* had a brief respite when she was reactivated for the war in 1914 and used as a bombardment ship off the Belgian coast. Her guns however were out-dated and had a limited range compared to the newer vessels – but her crew evolved a clever way of increasing the range. Torpedo bulges had been fitted to her hull along both sides as a protection against torpedo strikes and mines. The crew would flood a torpedo bulge along one side of the hull with seawater. This caused the ship to list over to that side and so lifted the other side of the ship higher, increasing the elevation of her guns and thus achieving a greater range. When stocks of the old specification 13.5-inch shells for her main guns ran out, her guns were relined to 12-inch. This increased their effective range to 16,000 yards. In the rush to arm for war however, the Admiralty could not afford to have precious crews and facilities tied up in keeping a ship afloat that had only a very limited potential use.

The development of effective submarines was comparatively recent, but the potential threat from German submarines was understood and greatly feared. The Admiralty were also aware that Germany had embarked on an intensive submarine construction programme earlier that year which would double their number of U-boats by the end of 1914. And so, the once proud *Hood* was earmarked to end her days by being scuttled as a block ship across the southern entrance to Portland Harbour. She would seal this entrance to prevent U-boats penetrating into the harbour itself, or lurking outside the harbour entrance and firing torpedoes into the harbour at the Channel Fleet anchored within.

On the day of her scuttling, *Hood* was towed into her assigned position – she was to be sunk at Slack Water to ensure she ended up correctly sealing the entrance. Her seacocks were opened, the idea being to allow her to sink gracefully and proudly in an upright position. Her pace of sinking however, turned out to be too slow and the tide turned. Soon, the strong tide was pulling her out of position. Explosives were hurriedly used to blow a hole in her side, and once she was blown open, huge volumes of water rushed into her. Battleships were renowned for their instability once flooded, most turning turtle as they sank. The inrushing waters soon caused *Hood* to roll to her port side and then turn upside down and sink quickly to the seabed. Although things had not gone quite to plan, with a depth of just 2 metres over her upturned keel, she very effectively

eliminated any clandestine entry into the harbour and any torpedo being fired at ships inside the harbour.

Nearly 90 years later, she still rests in position at the southernmost entrance to the harbour, still blocking it to navigation for any craft bigger than small boats. She lies in 18 metres with her shallowest upturned hull just 2 metres beneath the surface. Her bow and stern rest on the opposing piles of large concrete blocks that form the foundations for the two southernmost piers. Just forward of the bridge superstructure on the edge of the hull is a large sloping section where her anchors were lifted up onto instead of the more traditional type of hawse pipe arrangement. Either side of her superstructure, portholes, doorways and secondary gun emplacements can be made out. At her stern, although her propellers have been removed free sections of shaft are still visible and her large rudder still stands in place. Her main gun turrets were removed prior to her being scuttled.

In 2004 Portland Harbour Authority placed a temporary ban on diving HMS *Hood* due to large swell conditions through the entrance, increasing depth and the deteriorating condition of the wreck.

Shipwreck – the essentials	
Type of wreck	Royal Sovereign R Class battleship
Nationality	British
Launched	1891
Dimensions	410 ft x 75 ft x 27.5 ft
Displacement	14,150 tons design. 15,588 tons combat load.
Date sunk	4 November 1914
Cause of sinking	scuttled
Depth of water	18 metres
Least depth above wreck	2 metres
Position	50° 34.08N, 002° 25.12W

SS Maine.

SS MAINE, SALCOMBE, SOUTH DEVON

The 3,616-grt SS *Sierra Blanca* was laid down in 1904 by D. & W. Henderson, Shipbuilders, in Partick, Scotland for the Sierra Shipping Co Ltd. She was launched in January 1905 and completed in July that year. She was 375 ft in length had a beam of 46 ft. In 1913 she was sold to the Atlantic Transport Co Ltd of Liverpool and renamed the *Maine*.

In March 1917, the *Maine* was berthed in London's East India Dock, loading up with a small general cargo bound for Philadelphia, where she would collect a precious cargo of war supplies to take back to Britain.

On the other side of the English Channel, in the early hours of 17 March 1917, *UC-17*, under the command of Oberleutnant Ralph Wenniger, left her base at Zeebruge, about 50 miles north of Dunkirk, in the safety of the darkness. She was loaded with seven torpedoes and a complement of mines, with orders to proceed to Beachy Head and thereafter to Newhaven to lay mine barrages.

Two days after leaving Zeebruge, and having successfully laid mines at Beachy Head, near Eastbourne, *UC-17* surfaced close to the small French fishing vessel *Rhodona*. A boarding-party opened her seacocks and sent her to the bottom after allowing the crew to abandon ship to the lifeboats.

UC-17 then moved to Newhaven and completed the rest of her mission, laying the remainder of her mines there. She then moved further down the English Channel towards Start Point, sinking the fishing vessel *Curlew* with grenades on the way. She fired a torpedo at the 2,933-ton steamer *Huntscape* but missed. The following day she came across the 11,130-ton New Zealand steamship *Rotorua* – en route from Wellington, New Zealand to London with a large cargo – and successfully torpedoed and sunk her.

As dawn of 23 March 1917 broke, the SS *Maine* was about 13 miles south of Berry Head, in South Devon, approaching the western end of the English Channel as she headed for the open Atlantic. If she could slip through the Channel unscathed and break into the Atlantic then she would be relatively safe from U-boat attack. As they were in dangerous waters, special lookouts had been placed around the ship, continuously searching for the feared tell-tale wake of a periscope or the track of a torpedo. Meantime the *Maine* zigzagged to confuse any stalking U-boat.

Shipwreck – the essentials	
Type of wreck	steamship
Nationality	British
Launched	January 1905
Dimensions	375 ft x 46 ft
Tonnage	3,616 grt
Date sunk	23 March 1917
Cause of sinking	torpedo from *UC-17*
Depth of water	34 metres
Least depth above wreck	26 metres
Position	50° 12.82N, 003° 51.01W

The wreck of SS Maine off Bolt Head, South Devon.

© Rod Macdonald

But all these precautions were in vain, for at 8.05 a.m., a torpedo from *UC-17* slammed into the port side of the ship, just forward of the bridge at No. 2 hold. The force of the explosion blew the covers for hatches 2 and 3 right off, and the bridge was partially wrecked. The captain ordered that the presence of a U-boat be reported by radio, rockets and signal flags to other vessels nearby. He then altered course and started heading for land to try and save his stricken ship: the explosion had not affected the engine room.

After struggling a dozen miles towards land, seawater reached the stokehold and her engines had to be stopped. The *Maine* slowed and wallowed to a halt, rocking gently in the short seas. All efforts to take her in tow failed, and at 12.45 p.m., upright and on an even keel, some two and a half miles north-west of Bolt Head, the *Maine* succumbed to the sea. As the sea finally closed over her, her captain and remaining crew calmly stepped into a dingy that had been made ready, and floated off. Once she had settled on the bottom, both her 100-ft tall foremast and mainmast projected some 12 ft clear of the water at low tide.

Commercial salvers worked the *Maine* in the post war years. Her superstructure was blown off and dumped on the seabed nearby, allowing standard-dress divers to get at the valuable non-ferrous engine room fitments. In 1961 she was bought by the Torbay branch of the British Sub Aqua Club.

Today the wreck sits on an even keel on a white sandy seabed in an area renowned for good visibility. Her bow area retains its vast dominating shape although the foc'stle deck itself has rotted away. The hatches for her foredeck holds are still visible before the scars of the salvage work become evident – the centre of the wreck has been opened up by salvers as the superstructure was removed and dumped on the seabed nearby. Her boilers and triple expansion engine lie amid the debris. Aft of her superstructure area her after deck reforms with its cargo hatches allowing access to the holds below. Her schooner stern is intact and distinctive although her propeller was salved in the 1960's. She remains a magnificent wreck to dive – vast in scale.

The schooner rigged SS Bretagne. *Photo courtesy of Stewart Butterfield & the Bristol Aerospace Sub Aqua Club*

SS *BRETAGNE*, BABBACOMBE BAY, EAST DEVON

The 1,382-grt schooner-rigged single screw steamship *Bretagne* was built in 1903 in the Norwegian city then known as Christiania, but now known as Oslo. She measured 231.6 ft in length, with a beam of 35.2 ft and a draft of 14.7 ft. In addition to her powerful engine, she could fly up to 2,000 square ft of sail from her two masts if needed, to increase her speed in favourable conditions, or should her engine be put out of use.

For the first ten years of her life, she served as a general workhorse of the sea, but then a few years into World War I, in 1916, she was requisitioned by the British Ministry of War Transport and fitted out with a stern defensive quick firing (QF) 12-pound gun. These stern defensive guns were fitted to merchant vessels once it became clear that U-boats were targeting unarmed vessels. They allowed ships to fire on enemy surface raiders, such as U-boats,

The wreck of SS Bretagne in Babbacombe Bay, East Devon.

© Rod Macdonald

whilst using their greater speed to make good an escape.

In August 1918 – just three months before the Armistice silenced the guns over the European battlefields – the *Bretagne* set off from Barry in Wales, laden with 2000 tons of steam coal, bound for the port of Rouen in France. Her routing would take her round the south-west tip of England and up and across the English Channel to the Baie de la Seine. Here she would pass Le Havre, before entering the River Seine itself and proceeding up the river to her final destination, the port of Rouen, nearly 35 miles upstream. This small compact steamer with its shallow draft was ideally suited to carry her valuable cargo of coal far upstream.

On Saturday, 10 August 1918, as *Bretagne* was making her way up the English Channel, her progress was slowed by thick fog six miles off Berry Head near Torbay. Suddenly, at about 10.30 a.m., the bows of the French steamship *Renée Marthe* loomed out of the fog at speed and sliced into the *Bretagne*'s starboard side hull at the aftmost hold. The sound of the collision was so loud that it was heard by the nearby Torbay boom-defence vessel – which promptly set off to the scene to investigate.

The *Renée Marthe* pulled away from the stricken *Bretagne*, and this allowed tons of water to start flooding into the hull of the stricken steamer. It was then found that *Bretagne*'s steering was jammed to starboard, making it impossible to steer towards shore.

The Torbay boom-defence vessel arrived on the scene and Captain Johannesson – in charge of the *Bretagne* – accepted a tow. As that was being set up, most of the crew were taken off to safety however Captain Johannesson stayed aboard with his first mate and a naval gunner. The three men desperately tried to uncouple the jammed steering gear as with her rudder jammed to starboard she couldn't be towed in a straight line.

Bretagne was settling deeper and deeper into the water as the three men worked at the steering gear. When waves started washing over the decks, Captain Johannesson ordered his two remaining men into a lifeboat. The

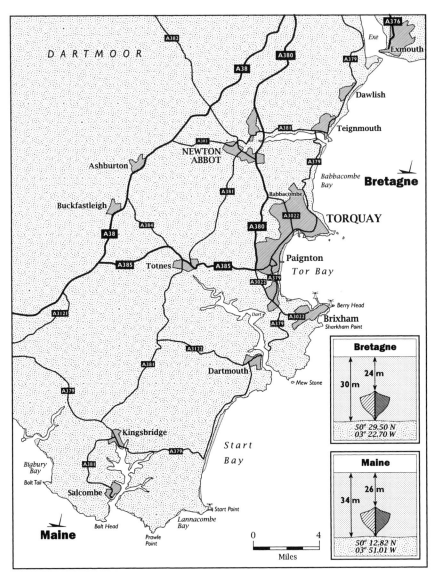

Location chart for SS Maine & SS Bretagne.

first mate however decided at the last minute to go back down below deck to try to save his personal possessions and money. Sadly he had left it too late: a wave swept over the deck and slammed a door behind him shut. He was trapped and unable to get back out before the *Bretagne* sank – and took him with it into the depths.

Today, the wreck of the *Bretagne* sits on an even keel in 30 metres of water a few miles offshore from Teignmouth in Babbacombe Bay. She is one of East Devon's most popular wrecks, and being relatively intact, she can easily be explored in one dive. Her straight stem is covered with sea life and is a magnificent sight. Her two foredeck holds are open for exploration – black, ominous, seemingly bottomless pits still filled with her cargo of coal. Her bridge superstructure is largely collapsed but aft of that, a pitched roof and skylights allow glimpses into the engine room.

On her starboard side at the aftmost hold, the gash where the bows of the *Renée Marthe* sliced into her can be clearly made out. The spare propeller sits secured on the deck, just in front of the now empty defensive gun platform – the gun itself was salvaged in the 1970s.

The unique 6-bladed propellers designed for the SS Kyarra.

SS *KYARRA*, ISLE OF PURBECK, DORSET

The 6,953-grt *Kyarra* was a beautiful twin-masted schooner-rigged steamer built on the River Clyde, Scotland, in 1902 and launched on 2 February 1903. She was an impressive 415 ft 5 in. in length, with a beam of 52 ft 2 in. and a draft of 31 ft 4.5 in. She was built to carry both cargo and fare-paying passengers and was fitted out with 42 first-class three-berth cabins, 20 second-class cabins of eight berths each, and a number of well-appointed state rooms. *Kyarra* spent the majority of her pre-war years carrying cargo and passengers around Australian shores and she became popular with Queensland and Western Australia passengers.

After ten years of profitable service, World War I unleashed itself across Europe, and in October 1914, the British Government requisitioned *Kyarra*. She was fitted out as a hospital ship, her hull painted white with large red crosses.

On 5 December 1914, she sailed from Australia for the European battlegrounds with five fully equipped medical units aboard for deployment under the control of Australian officers and crew. On reaching

Shipwreck – the essentials	
Type of wreck	schooner rigged steamship
Nationality	Norwegian
Launched	1903
Dimensions	231.6 ft x 35.2 ft x 14.7 ft
Tonnage	1305 grt
Date sunk	10 August 1918
Cause of sinking	rammed by SS *Renée Marthe*
Depth of water	30 metres
Least depth above wreck	24 metres
Position	50° 29.50N, 003° 22.70W

Shipwreck – the essentials

Type of wreck	steamship
Nationality	British
Launched	2 February 1903
Dimensions	415.5 ft x 52.2 ft x 31.2 ft
Tonnage	6,953-grt
Date sunk	26 May 1918
Cause of sinking	torpedo from *UB-57*
Depth of water	30 metres
Least depth above wreck	25 metres
Position	50°34 .90N, 001° 56.59W

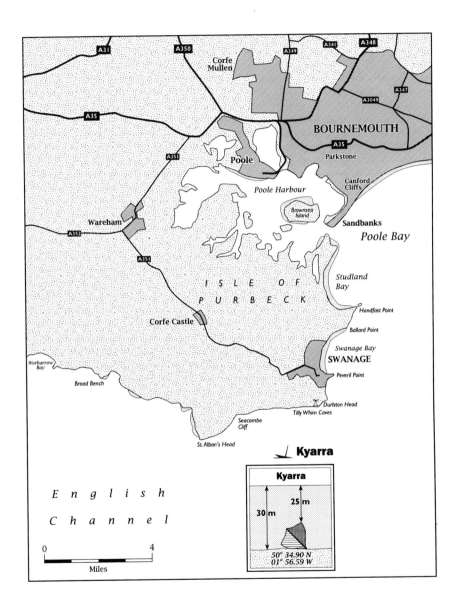

Location chart for the SS Kyarra.

Alexandretta, on the Turkish eastern side of the Mediterranean, shore hospitals were established and she then returned to Australia carrying wounded troops. She subsequently made several trips to Britain carrying cargo, before being involved in the landing of Anzac Expeditionary troops during the Gallipoli offensive of 1915/16. She went on to make several subsequent trips to Britain carrying cargo, before returning to Australia for the last time just before Christmas 1917.

On 8 February 1918, she set off from Melbourne on a voyage back to Britain, crossing the Pacific to the west coast of Central America before passing through the Panama Canal. From Panama she made her way up the east coast of America and headed out across the open waters of the Atlantic for Britain. She arrived in London safely in early May 1918, where lading started of 2,500 tons of general cargo to be shipped back to Australia, along with 1,000 war-wounded Australian service personnel who she was to embark at Devonport, Plymouth.

In the early hours of 23 May 1918, the German submarine *UB-57* was on patrol in the English Channel and had taken up a waiting position on the surface, not far from the Owers Lightship, off Sussex. Just before dawn,

The wreck of the SS Kyarra, Isle of Purbeck, Dorset.

UB-57 successfully torpedoed and sunk the troopship *Moldavia* (page 59). Despite extensive depth-charging by Royal Navy escort vessels, *UB-57* was able to slip away undetected to continue her patrol.

On the morning of 26 May 1918, *UB-57* was patrolling off Anvil Point near Swanage, when the unfortunate *Kyarra* crossed her path on the first leg of her journey from London to Devonport to collect the Australian war wounded for repatriation. Unseen, *UB-57* fired a single torpedo at *Kyarra*'s port side.

On *Kyarra*, the routine of shipboard life was suddenly shattered as one of the lookouts spotted the tell-tale track and shouted: "Torpedo approaching on the port side!" There was no time to react before the torpedo stuck her midships in the vicinity of the engine room, just forward of the boilers. The explosion killed five crew members instantly.

Almost immediately, *Kyarra* started to settle by the bow. Her engines had been put out of action by the explosion and she slewed to a wallowing stop. The order to abandon ship was given and the lifeboats were quickly winched out. *Kyarra* sank quickly by the bow. Just 20 minutes after the torpedo had struck, her stern lifted out of the water and she made her final plunge to the bottom. Thankfully, she had not yet embarked the 1,000 wounded Australian troops.

Today, the wreck of the *Kyarra* lies on her starboard side and is in quite an advanced state of collapse although she still retains her basic ship shape, with her keel and hull still recognisable. At the very stern, her rudder has fallen from its mounts to the seabed. Moving forward, the upper port side of the hull is collapsing down and a section of the portside hull lies flat on top – studded with portholes and a doorway. The main mast lies fallen to the seabed nearby. The

Right: The opulent boat deck of SS Kyarra.

Below: The 6,953-ton SS Kyarra in her fitting out dock on the River Clyde.

rims of the aft cargo hold hatches can be made out with cargo winches dotted here and there.

The midships superstructure is well collapsed and almost unrecognisable but forward of this area the ship regains its shape with the cargo hatches again visible and the foremast fallen to the seabed. The very tip of the bow with its chain locker, forward of the collision bulkhead, has detached itself from the main section of the wreck and lies on its starboard side .

THE US LIBERTY SHIP *JAMES EAGAN LAYNE*, WHITSAND BAY, CORNWALL

The wreck of the American Liberty ship *James Eagan Layne* is perhaps one of the most famous in British diving. She sits on her keel in relatively shallow water of 24 metres in Whitsand Bay, Cornwall, about three quarters of a mile offshore with a least depth down to her decks of just 10 metres.

'Liberty ships' were American standard ships: ships that were built to a standard design in huge numbers and at great speed to combat the loss of Allied shipping to U-boat activity in World War II. Liberty ships like *James Eagan Layne* played a vital role in the winning of the Battle of the Atlantic. Without them, the Allies would not have been able to ship sufficient quantities of war supplies to Great Britain. There would have been no D-day – and perhaps no Allied victory.

The Liberty shipbuilding programme started in 1940, at a time when America had not yet entered the war and Britain stood alone against the might of the German war machine. It was the 'happy time' for U-boats – a time when the U-boats were sinking British ships faster than replacement ships could be turned out by the British yards. In the first nine months of the war alone, 150 British ships were sent to the bottom – most victims of U-boat attack.

Britain had insufficient natural resources of her own and so the British war effort depended on imports of materials and vital products like oil.

With the high rate of shipping losses, Britain was slowly bleeding to death and would soon be powerless to defend herself. In her time of need, in September 1940, she turned to the might of America for help.

The Americans agreed to help, and initially a 200-ship construction programme got underway. The ships were constructed to a standard design, the aim being to try and build these ships in much the same way as a car assembly line. As many parts as possible would be independently prefabricated – such as superstructures and hull sections – before being assembled. The ships were all welded, as opposed to the older, more laborious, process of plates being drilled and riveted. Full size wooden templates were used for cutting out sections of steel. All had standard oil-fired engines.

The first Liberty ship was launched early in September 1941. On 27 September 1941 alone, 14 new ships were launched: the day itself was christened Liberty Day.

Two months later, America joined the war and President Roosevelt famously declared that, to beat the U-boat menace, America would build a 'Bridge of Ships' over the Atlantic. The aim was brutally simple: to mass-produce ships faster than they could be sunk. It would be a war of attrition: the whole nation was galvanised as ship production moved into a different gear and stepped up sharply.

New shipyards were built up and down America's coasts, and a huge number of shipyard workers were recruited from farms and other walks of life right across the country. The first Liberty ships under the new regime took just 150 days to build and 95 to equip. These ships were considered expendable and just one single successful transatlantic crossing justified the construction costs of up to $2,000,000 per ship. They were only made for the one trip – anything more was a bonus.

The Americans went on to develop and hone their production systems and the build-rate improved dramatically. By 1942, the fastest build had been cut to an almost incredible 47 days. In 1942 and 1943, some 1,500 Liberty ships were mass-produced: in 1944, some 800 more. The record

The wreck of the American Liberty ship James Eagan Layne *in Whitsand Bay, Cornwall.*

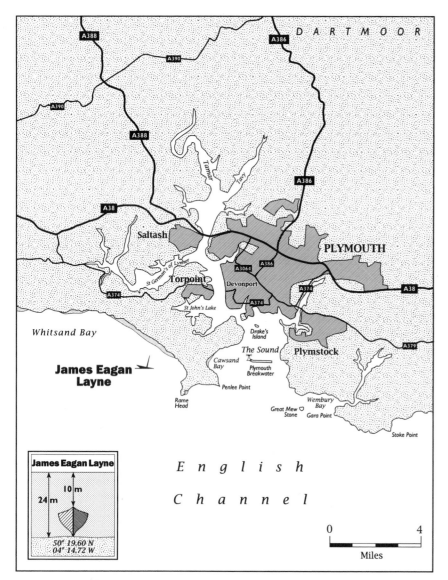

Location chart for the American WWII Liberty ship James Eagan Layne.

for completion of a single ship tumbled from 47 days to a staggering 15 days, then to 10 days, and soon to just 7 days from laying down her keel to completion. That same year, the fastest Liberty ship build was completed: the *Robert E. Peary* was launched in an amazing 4 days and 15 hours after her keel was laid. Three days later, it was on its way to collect its cargo. The huge American shipbuilding programme, which in all produced 2,700 Liberty ships, saved Britain in the Battle of the Atlantic.

The 7,176-grt *James Eagan Layne* was built in late 1944 at the Delta Shipbuilding Co. in New Orleans for the United States War Shipping Administration. She was 422.8 ft in length with a beam of 57 ft and draft of 34.8 ft. Her keel was laid down on 23 October 1944, and just 40 days later, on 2 December 1944, she was launched sideways into the Mississippi. It took just 16 days to kit her out before she was ready for delivery. She had five cavernous holds, three forward and two aft and a top speed of 11 knots. Her career at sea, however, would be cut almost as short as the time it took to build her – a brief 3 months.

After delivery, *James Eagan Layne* crossed the Atlantic to Britain, where she soon found herself berthed at the southern Welsh port of Barry, which opens onto the north side of the Bristol Channel. Her five huge holds were filled with a general war cargo that included tank parts, jeeps, lorries and railway rolling stock intended for General Patton's Third Army, whose tanks were racing across Europe towards the Rhine.

The *James Eagan Layne* headed west out of the Bristol Channel on 20 March (as lead ship of the starboard column of convoy BTC-103) before turning southwards and running down the northern shores of Devon and Cornwall. Turning at Land's End, the most south-westerly point of the mainland, the convoy headed north-east up the English Channel. On 21 March 1945, the convoy was approaching Plymouth. Here *U-399*, a Type VIIC U-boat, lurked unseen.

At about 1.35pm *U-399* fired a torpedo which struck the unsuspecting *James Eagan Layne* on her starboard side just aft of the bulkhead between hold No's 4 & 5. The explosion threw a large plume of water high into the air, blew off the cover for No 5 hatch and caused a crack in the portside from the water line to the bulwark rail and across the deck, aft of No 4 hatch. The stern was expected to break away. The engines were secured and the vessel slewed to a wallowing halt. A coded 'sub-attack' message was immediately sent off, and as *James Eagan Layne* lay dead in the water slowly sinking, Royal Navy frigates out of nearby Plymouth arrived on the scene and set about depth-charging the unseen enemy.

Simultaneously, two Admiralty tugs HMS *Flaunt* and HMS *Atlas* arrived on the scene and attached towing hawsers in an attempt to get her to Plymouth and save her vital war cargo. But it soon became clear that she would not remain afloat long enough to reach the port, and so the tow was redirected to Whitsand Bay where it was hoped she could be run aground on the soft sandy seabed. She was down by the stern when, at about 7pm she grounded by the stern not far offshore in 22 metres of water. She was then secured in place by anchors and chains. A day later the Admiralty Salvage Officer reported that the aft holds were freely flooding but that the forward holds were still dry and the engine room only had seven feet of water in it.

On 24 March however, the after engine room bulkhead gave way causing flooding of the engine room. With the ship flooded up to No 3 hatch she finally settled on the bottom with her upper superstructures showing at low water and only her masts and funnel showing at high water. Some cargo was immediately salved from the forward section of the ship whilst it was still dry and her guns and deck cargo were removed. In 1953 salvage operations started which removed most of the remaining cargo.

Today, the wreck of this famous Liberty ship sits on an even keel in 22 metres of water. Being so close to Plymouth and in such shallow water, she is regularly visited by divers. The uppermost tip of her bow lies just 5 metres beneath the surface and the cavernous spaces of the three foredeck holds are ideal training areas – although the deck structure has collapsed in recent years. The decking and internal bulkheads have rotted away to leave a latticework of her structure and frames.

Midships, her triple-expansion engine still stands upright in the remains of the engine room. Aft of this area, where the torpedo struck, the hull loses its shape and has collapsed. The propeller shaft tunnel leads from the engine directly to the stern. The very stern of the ship has cracked and detached from the main section – the gap in between strewn with remnants of her wartime cargo.

Shipwreck – the essentials	
Type of wreck	Liberty ship
Nationality	American
Launched	2 December 1944
Dimensions	422.8 ft x 57 ft x 34.8 ft
Tonnage	7,176 grt
Date sunk	21 March 1945
Cause of sinking	torpedoed by *U-399*
Depth of water	24 metres
Least depth above wreck	10 metres
Position	50° 19.60N, 004° 14.72W

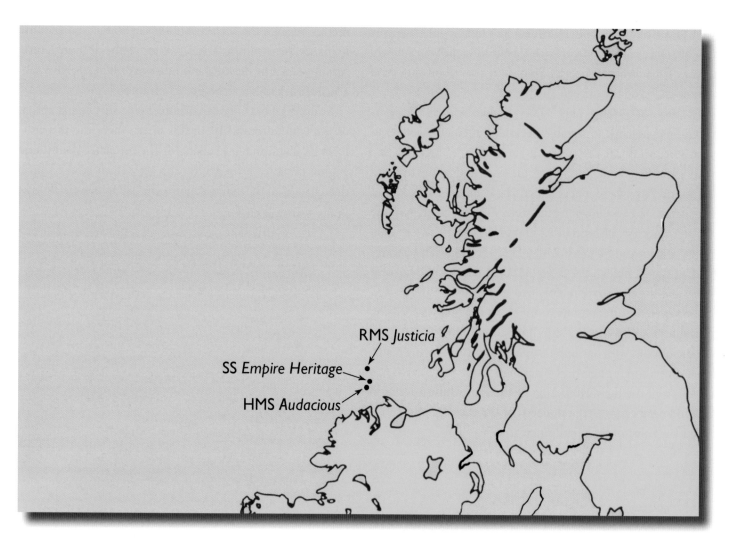

The famous wrecks of the North Channel, Irish Sea.

3

The NORTH CHANNEL, Irish Sea

THE WHITE STAR LINER *JUSTICIA*, MALIN HEAD

The wreck of the massive 32,234-ton Royal Mail Ship RMS *Justicia* lies on a clean white sandy bottom in 70 metres of crystal clear Atlantic water, 25 miles out from Malin Head, Co Donegal, where average underwater visibility is in the region of 50 metres. She is massive in scale – 756 ft long with a beam of 86 ft. Her bows are of the size and scale of the *Titanic's*.

In the early years of the 20th century, opulent shipping lines competed to offer the largest and fastest ocean liners to win custom from discerning transatlantic passengers. The great ships of the era are still household names today: *Titanic, Laurentic, Britannic, Olympic* and many others.

The Dutch, Holland-Amerika Line, had enviously eyed the dominance of the great British shipping lines such as White Star and Cunard and wanted similar great ships as emblem bearers, not just for their shipping line, but also to represent their nation. They approached the legendary firm of Harland & Wolff in Belfast – builders of the *Titanic* – with an order for a new 32,234-ton liner.

The keel of their new ship was laid down in 1912. Two years later, on 9 July 1914, the new ship was launched and named *Statendam*. Work immediately

The bows of the White Star liner Justicia, *the North Channel, Irish Sea © Barry McGill*

began on fitting her out for her planned entry into the lucrative North Atlantic run from Europe to the United States.

Just 11 days before her launch however, on 28 June 1914, Serb nationalist Gavrilo Princip assassinated the Austrian-Hungarian crown prince in Sarajevo and triggered World War I. The world that the *Statendam* had been conceived and built for disappeared overnight – before she had even carried a single commercial passenger. In September 1914, the Holland-Amerika Line was forced to stop the fitting out of the almost completed *Statendam*, and the ship lay idle into the following year.

In 1915, the unfinished and laid-up *Statendam* was requisitioned for war use and purchased by the British Government, who needed large, fast ships for use as troop carriers. The *Statendam*'s immense size and anticipated speed made her a perfect choice.

Harland & Wolff restarted work on the ship, but because of wartime material and labour shortages, progress was slow. To save sheet metal, the ship's funnels were made smaller in diameter than originally designed and this gave her a slightly odd appearance. It took Harland & Wolff until 7 April 1917 to complete the *Statendam*. Once she was fully ready for war use as a troopship - able to carry 4,000 troops - she was renamed *Justicia*.

The British Government intended *Justicia* to be a replacement for the *Lusitania* – which had infamously been torpedoed in 1915, with huge civilian loss of life. The Cunard shipping line would manage her during the war – and like all their liners, her name would end with '–ia'. Once the war was won, ownership would be passed outright by the government to Cunard.

However, by the time of her completion in 1917, Cunard found itself unable to muster a full crew for her. The Admiralty wanted *Justicia* in war service as soon as possible and could not wait for Cunard to solve the crew problem. Accordingly, the Admiralty offered *Justicia* for wartime management to Cunard's rival, the White Star Line, because they had the crew of the recently sunk *Britannic* available. In 1918, *Justicia*'s grey hull was painted in a dazzle pattern, designed to confuse its silhouette for any enemy raiders observing her from a distance.

After more than a year of war service, on 19 July 1918, *Justicia* set off on a voyage from Belfast to New York. Not far into the voyage – just 23 miles south of the tiny rocky outcrop of Skerryvore lighthouse (12 miles south of the southernmost tip of the west coast island of Tiree in Scotland) – she was attacked and successfully torpedoed by *UB-64*.

Justicia took on a list as seawater poured into her hull through the plating torn open by the single torpedo strike – but her watertight compartments successfully contained the water in the damaged area and stopped her from completely flooding and sinking. Royal Navy destroyers were summoned to escort her to safe waters, and she turned to run for the Irish mainland and safety.

However, *UB-64* had not finished with *Justicia*, pressing home her attack despite the protecting destroyers. She skilfully manoeuvred into another attacking position and fired two more torpedoes, which struck *Justicia*'s side, blowing open two more huge gashes in her hull. Even this additional damage was not enough to send the massive liner to the bottom: again, her watertight compartments held and kept her afloat. Most of the crew were taken off the ship, with only a small number of essential hands being left aboard.

Justicia's engines now had to be stopped because of the water flooding into her hull from the two further torpedo strikes. The tug HMS *Sonia* attached a cable and started a tow for Lough Swilly, where the water was shallow enough to beach her safely.

UB-64 continued to stalk the stricken liner however, determined to send her to the bottom. A few hours further into the tow, she fired a fourth torpedo into the labouring liner. This time, *UB-64* was damaged by Royal Navy escort vessels and was finally forced to break off the attack. The tow to Lough Swilly resumed.

As it left the scene, *UB-64* reported *Justicia*'s position and condition to German command and another U-boat – *UB-124* – was ordered to take over the hunt. *UB-124* caught up with *Justicia* the following day, 20 July 1918.

Left: The massive White Star liner Justicia.

Above right: The Justica *dazzle painted during World War I.*

Above: The wreck of the White Star liner RMS Justica.

At 9 a.m. that morning, *UB-124* had *Justicia* in her sights and successfully fired two torpedoes. *Justicia* was already severely damaged from the previous day's four torpedoes from *UB-64* – these two further strikes proved too much for her. By noon, she had listed well over onto her side and shortly afterwards she finally succumbed to the sea, with 16 men from the engine room lost.

UB-124 was detected and attacked with depth-charges by the destroyers *Marne*, *Milbrook* and *Pigeon*. Damaged, she was forced to the surface and abandoned by her crew. German sources report that her crew scuttled her, whilst British sources report she was sunk by naval gunfire. Either way, she went to the bottom with all bar two of her crew being saved and taken prisoner.

After just over one year of service – and having never carried a single paying passenger – *Justicia* was gone.

Today, the massive wreck of *Justicia* sits in the midst of a clean, white, sandy desert in about 70 metres of water. The most photogenic part of her is the large *Titanic*-style bow section which, even though well sunk into the seabed, rises up from 70 metres to about 55 metres and is slightly canted over to port. On the starboard side, her anchor still is held snug in its hawse – the chain running up through the hawse pipe to the fo'c'stle deck. The port-side anchor is also still in position, but not so visible. At the very tip of her bow, guardrails still ring around the deck. The anchor chains run back along the deck to huge capstans which, because the bow is collapsing, have been thrust up through the deck.

Aft of the chain locker and collision bulkhead, the foredeck area has collapsed down almost flat – pulverised by Atlantic storms. The whole structure of the main section of the wreck has collapsed and fallen towards the port side, and the square fronted bridge superstructure lies on the sand to the port side.

Aft of the bridge, the wreck is flattened and opened up, with sections of the riveted starboard side lying over it. Rows of massive exposed Scotch boilers, each one the size of a small house, lead back towards the engine rooms where the triple-expansion engines that turned the two outer propellers can be located near the exhaust-steam turbine which turned the centre propeller.

Shipwreck – the essentials	
Type of wreck	White Star passenger liner
Nationality	British
Launched	7 April 1917
Dimensions	776 ft x 86 ft
Tonnage	32,234 grt
Date sunk	20 July 1918
Cause of sinking	torpedoed by *UB-64* and *UB-124*
Depth of water	70 metres
Least depth above wreck	60 metres
Position	55º 39. 45N, 007º 43.15W

HMS AUDACIOUS, MALIN HEAD

The 598-foot King George V class battleship HMS *Audacious* has the dubious honour of being the first British battleship to be sunk during World War I – on 27 October 1914. The story of the loss of HMS *Audacious* also involves a famous White Star liner, RMS *Olympic*, which would carry out a dramatic rescue attempt.

Audacious was laid down at Birkenhead, Merseyside in March 1911, launched on 14 September 1912 and commissioned in August 1913. She was fitted with ten 13.5-inch guns set in five twin turrets, two super-firing forward A&B turrets, two super-firing aft X&Y turrets and one midships Q turret. Sixteen 4-inch secondary guns were set eight along either side mainly in casemate mounts at the time of her construction but these proved ineffectual and they were removed and substituted with 12 deck mounted 4-inch guns. Three 21-inch submerged torpedo tubes were fitted one in

© Rod Macdonald

The wreck of HMS Audacious.

Inset: 13.5-inch barbette © Barry McGill

either beam and a third in the stern. She was protected by 12-inch thick lower armour belt and 8-inch upper belt.

In 1914, due to the Admiralty's concern about the vulnerability of the U-boat defences at the British Grand Fleet's main base at Scapa Flow, the 2nd Battle Squadron of the British Grand Fleet spent the first few months of the war based at Lough Swilly on the northern Irish coast whilst works were carried out to make Scapa Flow secure. The Germans were aware of the Grand Fleet's deployment to Lough Swilly and sent the converted liner *Berlin* to lay a minefield in the shipping areas outside the Lough. This minefield was intended to strike at British merchant shipping, as well as the Grand Fleet.

Above: The British battleship HMS Audacious.

Right: The stern of HMS Audacious, the North Channel, Irish Sea © Barry Mcgill

Inset: A secondary 4" gun lies upturned on the seabed beside the wreck © Barry McGill

The upturned stern and twin rudders of HMS Audacious © Grainne Patton

On 27 October 1914, the 2nd Battle Squadron consisting of the super dreadnoughts *King George V, Ajax, Centurion, Monarch, Thunderer, Orion* and *Audacious* left Lough Swilly to conduct gunnery exercises. At 8.50 a.m., in the middle of a turn *Audacious* struck one of the *Berlin's* mines off Tory Island. The mine exploded under the ship at the rear of the port engine room, which had soon flooded – along with the machine room, X turret shell room and compartments below them. The ship soon had taken on a list of 10-15 degrees to port. Thinking that a U-boat had attacked his ship, the Captain hoisted the submarine warning signal – and fearing a possible torpedo attack on the other ships of the fleet, Admiral John Jellicoe ordered the Grand Fleet to leave the area. The light cruiser HMS *Liverpool*, and a number of smaller vessels would remain on the scene to assist the damaged battleship. Counter flooding of compartments on the opposite starboard side reduced the list. With the central and starboard side engine rooms still operating the ship could still make 9 knots.

Water continued to flood the ship however and at 10 a.m. the central engine room had to be abandoned – followed soon after by the starboard engine room being secured.

At 10.30 a.m., the captain of HMS *Liverpool* spotted the *Olympic* on a return crossing from New York – and ordered her to assist in the evacuation of the 900-strong crew of the *Audacious*. By 11 a.m., as *Audacious* rolled with the swell, her port side main deck was dipping under the water. Two hours later, all but 250 of the battleship's crew had been taken off, and arrangements had been agreed to take the damaged battleship in tow to safety.

The small and nimble destroyer HMS *Fury* set up a cable between *Audacious* and the larger and more powerful *Olympic*, and by 2 p.m., the tow was ready to start. Initially, progress was encouraging and the *Olympic* slowly started to make way, pulling the sluggish weight of *Audacious* westwards towards safety - flanked by the other ships of the rescue party. But when *Olympic* was required to alter course to SSE, to head towards Lough Swilly, things began to unravel. The seas were starting to rise and as the steering gear of *Audacious* was no

longer operational, she became increasingly unmanageable. Eventually, she sheared off into the wind and the towline parted.

Another attempt at a tow was made at 3.30 p.m., this time by the light cruiser HMS *Liverpool*. HMS *Fury* once again succeeded in attaching a cable, but after only 15 minutes, it became fouled in the cruiser's propellers, and it too parted.

By 4 p.m., *Audacious* was well down into the water with only 4 feet clear at the bow and one foot clear at the stern. HMS *Fury* took over a third tow-cable for yet another attempt. But as this cable was being tightened, it broke. *Olympic* was ordered to stand by and be ready to make another attempt.

By 5 p.m., the quarterdeck of the *Audacious* was awash and the decision was made to evacuate the majority of the crew who had remained on board. During the crew evacuation, due to the heavy weather and deteriorating conditions aboard *Audacious*, it was decided to abandon her completely until the next morning. By 6.30 p.m., the entire crew of the stricken battleship had been safely taken aboard *Olympic* and HMS *Liverpool*.

At 8.55 p.m., *Audacious* turned turtle and floated upside down until about 9 p.m., when there was a massive explosion in the vicinity of the forward magazines, which served A and B turrets. Within minutes, the battleship sank stern first.

For security reasons, the Admiralty tried to cover up the sinking, but despite their best attempts, speculation crept into the public domain. In an effort to hide the disaster, the Admiralty went as far as modifying the SS *Mountclan* to resemble the lost battleship. But the large number of witnesses to the sinking, many photographs and the inevitable loose tongues made the task of keeping the secret all but impossible. It proved difficult enough to persuade the neutral passengers who had been aboard the *Olympic* during the attempts to save the battleship to keep silent, but some of the crew themselves also let the cat out of the bag.

The only casualty during the entire momentous incident was the unfortunate petty officer, William Burgess, on HMS *Liverpool*. He was sadly killed while standing on the deck of the cruiser, some 800 yards away, when he

The 13.5-inch guns of B turret HMS Audacious, North Channel © Barry McGill

HMS Audacious *in tow behind HMS* Liverpool.

Shipwreck – the essentials

Type of wreck	King George V-class battleship
Nationality	British
Launched	14 September 1912
Dimensions	598 ft x 89 ft x 28 ft
Displacement	23,400 tons
Date sunk	27 October 1914
Cause of sinking	mine
Depth of water	67 metres
Least depth above wreck	60 metres
Position	55 28.29N, 007 45.10W

was hit by a 2 ft x 3 ft fragment of armour plate as *Audacious* blew up. The decks of the cruiser had been crowded, so it was perhaps fortunate that no one else was killed or injured.

Today, the wreck of HMS *Audacious* lies upside down in 67 metres of water on a clean white sandy bottom with underwater visibility usually in the region of 30-50 metres. The stern section is intact and in good condition, with her twin rudders still standing upright and her four high-speed propellers situated just forward of them.

The middle section of the battleship is largely intact although starting to sag – it is probably being supported by Q turret barbette. Near the bow however there is a scene of utter devastation. The hull stops abruptly in the vicinity of the conning tower and descends into a scattered debris field, with parts of ship, winches, secondary casemate guns, cordite propellant charges and 13.5-inch shells for the main guns all scattered around amidst sheared plates and sections of ship. Some 100 feet of the bow section is missing – blown off in the magazine explosion. The hull has been blown open and peeled back with such force that the very tip of the bow, still with its anchors in place, lies almost halfway back down the ship on the starboard side.

A massive 13.5-inch gun-turret lies upside down and detached from the wreck on one side, its twin 13.5-inch gun barrels lying flat on the sand. (cf the Cover photograph). The cylindrical barbette for B turret, some 45 feet across, lies upright and exposed on the seabed on the starboard side of the wreck.

Just aft of the foremost gun-turret sits a second upturned cylindrical feature – the bottom of the conning tower.

SS *Empire Heritage*, Malin Head

The 15,702grt SS *Empire Heritage* started her life at sea as the 512 feet long, 13,640-ton Antarctic whaling factory ship *Tafelberg*, which was built by Armstrong Whitworth & Co. Ltd in Newcastle upon Tyne in 1930. Her first name, *Tafelberg*, means "Table Mountain" in Dutch and Afrikaans. Her new owners were a South African seal and whaling company and her name referred to the famous mountain overlooking Cape Town. Being an Antarctic whaling factory ship she was fitted with a strengthened hull for working in ice and massive tanks for carrying whale oil. At the time of her launch, she was the largest factory ship in the world.

Nine years later, *Tafelberg* was still heading south for each whaling season when World War II erupted over Europe. By then, she was the pride of new owners – the shipping company Salveson's of Leith. Her tanks, designed for carrying whale oil, were ideally suited to carrying more valuable fuel oil and she had soon found a new role and in 1940, she is listed as returning to Britain from the US with a cargo of fuel oil. In January 1941, she struck a mine in the Bristol Channel and, badly damaged, became beached. After several weeks, she was refloated, but was grounded again at Whitmore Bay for temporary repairs. She became stuck on a sand bar, eventually breaking her back and splitting in two.

She was subsequently repaired and refloated and then requisitioned by the British Ministry of War Transport for conversion to an *Empire* ship. The prefix *Empire* denoted that she was one of 1,300 ships that were built or requisitioned by the Ministry of War Transport for war service. She was armed with six 20mm Oerlikon cannons, a 12-pounder gun and other anti aircraft weapons. By the time she was fully converted to an Empire ship her tonnage had increased to 15,702-tons. She was renamed *Empire Heritage* and returned to service in February 1943, taking part in several transatlantic supply convoys, as well as convoys to Egypt, Bombay and Aden.

In September 1944, she was berthed in Hoboken, New Jersey, on the other side of the Hudson River from Manhattan, New York. Beside her was

Sherman tank deck cargo, Empire Heritage © *Barry McGill*

Above: The massive boilers of the SS Empire Heritage © *Grainne Patton*

Right: Fine stern view of the whaler Tafelberg *before conversion to the* Empire Heritage.

another Salveson's of Leith ex-whaling factory ship requisitioned by the Ministry of Shipping and converted to transport crude oil, the *Empire Chief* – formerly known as the *Polar Chief*. Her crew were mostly seamen from the Highlands and Islands of Scotland – men from places like the Shetlands, Stornoway, North and South Uist: men with the sea in their blood. The two Salveson's crews were delighted to be in each other's company in such difficult times, to enjoy the camaraderie of the sea, exchange news and views – as well as a good dram. On the night of *Empire Chief*'s arrival, the two crews went out together in Hoboken, having dinner in the Clam Broth House and then cramming the bar. The drinking, singing and laughter went on until 3 or 4 in the morning. Every third drink was on the house – as was the custom at that time.

The next morning, the *Heritage* sailed, her off-watch crew lining the rails, waving and shouting to their new pals on the *Empire Chief*. She formed up as part of Convoy HX 305, along with 106 other merchant ships and naval escorts bound for Liverpool. She was the 4th ship in the 5th column. Her tanks were full of 16,000 tons of fuel oil and on her decks she carried a 1,947-ton deck cargo of trucks, general war supplies, Sherman tanks and dump trucks.

In the dead of night at 3.51 a.m. on 8 September 1944, as she approached Ireland, she was struck by a single torpedo on her starboard side from *U-482*, a Type VIIC U-boat. The explosion tore open one of her 9 tanks carrying fuel oil. There was then a secondary explosion as the fuel oil ignited. Heavily laden and running low in the water – as tankers were constructed to do – she went down so quickly that no flares could be fired or emergency signals sent, and many crew below decks had no time to escape from the ship. The factory deck was a massive open space that ran the full length of the ship - it was only 12–18 inches above the water line and would have flooded quickly, once opened to the sea by the torpedo. *Empire Heritage* rolled rapidly over onto her starboard side before completely capsizing within 2 minutes. By 3.56 a.m. – less than 5 minutes after the attack – she was gone, with the loss of 113 of her passengers and crew.

© Rod Macdonald

The pulverised remains of Empire Heritage, *her deck cargo of Sherman tanks and trucks tumbled to the seabed, lies in 68 metres in the North Channel, Irish Sea.*

Inset: The SS Empire Heritage (Tafelberg) *off Cape Town, South Africa.*

The stern, port propeller and rudder of the SS Empire Heritage, *North Channel, Irish Sea © Barry McGill*

The small Royal Fleet Auxiliary rescue vessel *Pinto*, following at the rear of the convoy, was detached - and exposing herself to great danger, stopped to pick up survivors from the *Empire Heritage*. Some of those survivors, whilst in the water, spotted 8 feet of a U-boat periscope sticking up through the water as it closed on the *Pinto*. As they watched, the periscope passed right through the survivors and wreckage before submerging as another Allied vessel approached.

Shortly afterwards, at 4.34 a.m., with the survivors now on board, *Pinto* herself was struck by a torpedo on her starboard side directly under the bridge. It was a devastating blow for such a small ship and she is reported to have sunk in 90 seconds. The unfortunate survivors of the *Empire Heritage* who had just been plucked to apparent safety were pitched back into the water for a second time in just 30 minutes. Some of them had in fact been aboard the *Empire Heritage* after their own convoy vessels had been sunk, and found themselves torpedoed for a third time. The wreck of the *Pinto* now lies just half a mile from the *Empire Heritage* – a poignant snapshot of the horrors of war.

Today the wreck of the *Empire Heritage* sits upright, but well pulverised by the might of the Atlantic storms – despite lying in 68 metres of water. At 512 ft long and 72 ft wide, she is a massive wreck.

The very stern section lies well rolled over to starboard with one of her two large propellers, the port-side propeller and free section of shaft, exposed. The rudder has fallen to the seabed nearby. The remainder of the wreck sits on its keel – having righted itself as it sank, but having subsequently collapsed to starboard. Her six massive boilers are now exposed – each one the size of a small house and sitting in two rows of three.

The deck cargo of Sherman tanks, half tracks and trucks, now lie clustered together in a jumble to starboard, some sitting upright on their tracks on the seabed; others upside down or on their side. All around, trucks lay strewn, their rotted remains easily identifiable from their rugged tyres.

Amidships, the large H-frame derrick still rises out of small deckhouses either side of the deck and stands 10 metres or more high. The bridge superstructure was set close to the very bow and is well collapsed and pulverised, as is the bow and foredeck itself.

Shipwreck - the essentials	
Type of wreck	Antarctic whaling factory ship/oil fuel tanker
Nationality	South Africa / requisitioned during WWII
Launched	1930
Dimensions	512 ft x 72.5 ft x 50.5 ft
Tonnage	15,702 grt
Date sunk	8 September 1944
Cause of sinking	torpedoed by U-482
Depth of water	68 metres
Least depth above wreck	60 metres
Position	55 32.5N, 007 43.0W

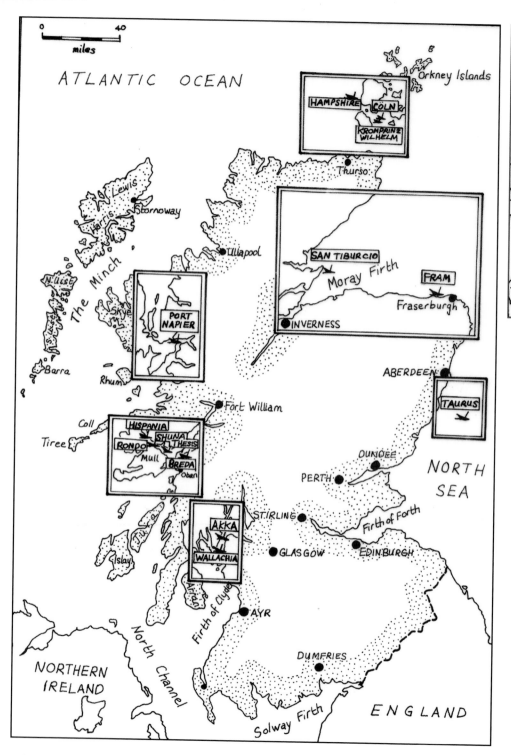

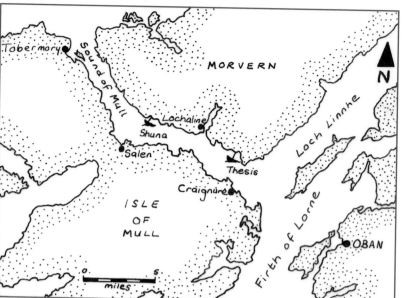

Above: Location chart for SS Shuna & SS Thesis.

Left: Location chart for Scottish shipwrecks.

4

WEST COAST OF SCOTLAND

SS *SHUNA*, SOUND OF MULL

The 1,426-grt steamship SS *Shuna* was built in 1909 in Holland and registered in Glasgow. A substantial steamer, she measured 240.9 ft in length with a beam of 35.2 ft and a draft of 16.5 ft. Just four years after her launch, on 8 May 1913, she was wrecked in the Sound of Mull on the west coast of Scotland.

In early May 1913, the *Shuna* set off on a voyage from Glasgow to Gothenburg in Sweden, with her holds full to the brim with a cargo of Welsh coal. Once she left the safety of the Firth of Clyde, she turned her head to the north and started running up the west coast of Scotland. The rugged islands of Islay and Jura passed by on her port beam. Shortly after, she ran into a heavy storm as she moved up the Firth of Lorne, passing Oban in the distance on her starboard beam.

After crossing Loch Linnhe in poor visibility, she moved towards the southern entrance to the Sound of Mull, the strip of water, some 15 miles long and a few miles across, that divides the eastern shores of the island of Mull from the west coast of mainland Scotland. It can offer a shortcut, sheltered from Atlantic storms, as an alternative to an often exposed and lengthy detour round the west coast of Mull, through the Passage of Tiree.

SS Shuna, *Sound of Mull.*

However, treacherous rocks, reefs and shoals – some barely submerged – await the unwary mariner. The Sound of Mull is a graveyard for countless vessels.

At about 10 p.m., navigating by dead reckoning and off course and too far to the north, disaster struck the *Shuna* near the southern entrance to

105

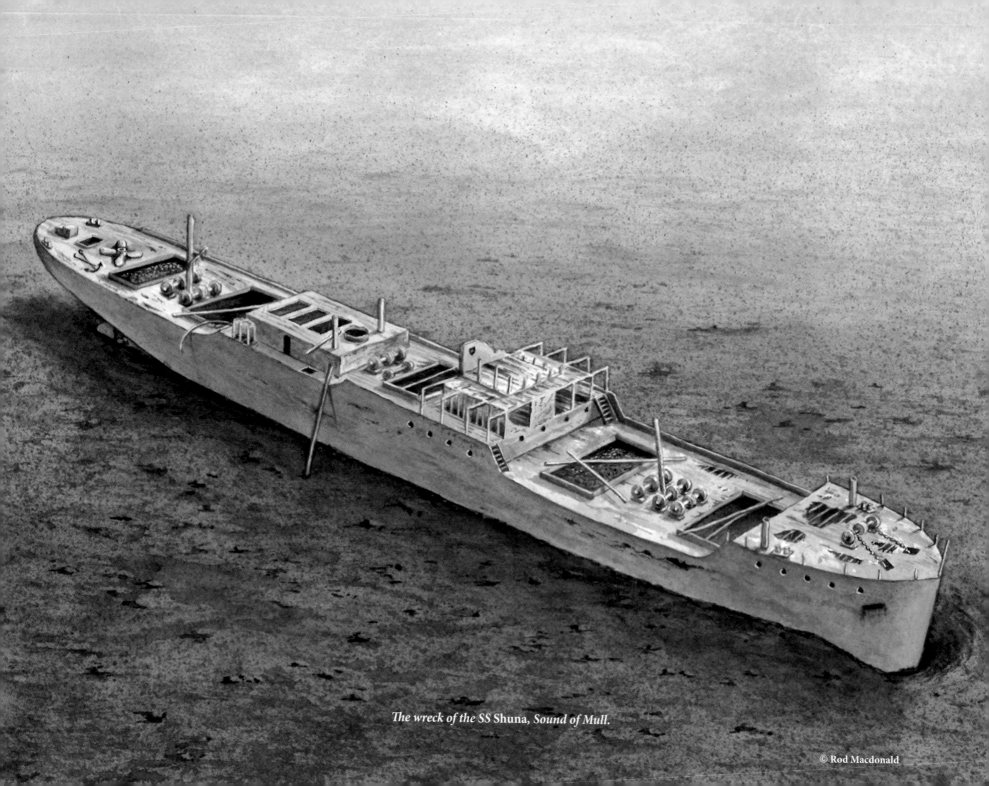

The wreck of the SS Shuna, Sound of Mull.

© Rod Macdonald

the Sound, when she ran onto the Gray Rocks – known in Gaelic as 'Liath Sgeir'. This dangerous islet lies just to the north-west of the southern tip of the large island of Lismore that guards the north side of the entrance. Rising up from depths of more than 65 metres to dry out by a height of only 3 metres at Low Water, at the weaker Neap tides it is usually mostly awash at High Water. At the stronger Spring tides, it is completely submerged – a hidden danger to shipping, just a few metres beneath the surface. But the part that dries out at low water is like the tip of an iceberg – a large part of Liath Sgeir is always submerged and would be a hazard to large ships such as the *Shuna*. The collision with the Gray Rocks rent open plating on the *Shuna*'s hull and she started to take on water. Her pumps were started and her captain decided to run for the protected anchorage of Tobermory at the north end of the Sound, some 15 miles away.

A couple of hours later, in the wee small hours of the night and some 11 miles into the journey north to Tobermory, it became clear that water was flooding into her faster than her pumps could handle: the plan had to be quickly changed. It was decided to beach her on the sheltered mainland shores of Morvern – six miles short of Tobermory – in the hope that she could be repaired and refloated. In the pitch darkness of the middle of the night, the captain chose a small bay just to the north of the Rubha Aird Seisg promontory. The die was cast for a desperate gamble.

As the *Shuna* drove in the darkness towards the shore of the bay, both anchors were let go to seaward, in the hope that once the she was repaired the anchors could be winched in and the *Shuna* pulled off the beach. The *Shuna*'s bow drove onto the shallow seabed of the shore and the ship shuddered to a halt. Unfortunately however, unknown to the captain, the sandy seabed in the bay that he had chosen drops away quite quickly down to a depth of more than 30 metres. Although the *Shuna*'s bows were aground, her stern was still afloat in quite a depth of water. The storm continued unabated and her stricken hull was battered by substantial waves. Water continued to flood through the gash in her hull and her stern settled lower and lower into the water as time went on.

A few hours later, the storm had begun to abate and with the seas settling, the captain sent the ship's mate up the Sound to Tobermory, on Mull, to summon assistance. As the crew waited, the *Shuna* settled even further into the water.

At 5 a.m., the next morning, dawn's early weak light revealed the *Shuna* in a desperate predicament. Her stern to midships had settled so deep in the water that the crew were forced to abandon ship. The lifeboats were run out and lowered from their davits atop the engine room.

The crew boarded the boats and rowed to the shore, just a few hundred metres away. A steel hawser was run out to the shore and secured in an attempt to hold her in the shallows.

At around 10 a.m., the water flooding into her hull had compressed the trapped air in her holds so much that the cargo hatches blew off. With this, the stern of the *Shuna* finally succumbed and slipped beneath the waves. The steel hawser secured to the shore snapped with the strain.

The stern settled on the bottom in about 20 metres of water, but as it was much deeper than the bow (which had grounded in just over five metres of water on the shallow beach) the ship started to slither down the underwater slope until the seabed finally bottomed out almost 200 metres offshore. Here the *Shuna* ground to a halt and settled on an even keel in about 30 metres of water.

Once she had disappeared from sight – just a few tens of metres from the crew on the shore – the crew got back into the lifeboats and rowed several miles up the Sound, reaching Tobermory around midday.

The wreck of the *Shuna* was then forgotten about and she lay in obscurity where she sank, her holds still full of her cargo of coal. Cloaked in the depths, she was lost to history for almost 80 years until, in the early 1990s, a local clam diver foraging for clams ran into a solid wall of rotted steel: a rusting but intact unknown shipwreck. The bell and brass letters on her fo'c'stle hull soon revealed her identity. The *Shuna* had been rediscovered.

Today, the wreck of the *Shuna* still lies in the small sheltered bay, bows obliquely pointing to the shore, just 200 metres away. She can be dived in

Shipwreck – the essentials

Type of wreck	steamship
Nationality	British
Launched	1909
Dimensions	240.9 ft x 35.2 ft x 16.5 ft
Tonnage	1,426 grt
Date sunk	8 May 1913
Cause of sinking	striking the Gray Rocks
Depth of water	32 metres
Least depth above wreck	18 metres
Position	55º 33.26N, 005º 54.52W

most weather states, either by boat or by a snorkel out from the shore. She sits on an even keel, somewhat settled into the seabed, and is structurally intact. Her sheer bow is magnificent: the stem dropping away vertically in the classic style of her era. Her fo'c'stle still has its anchor winch, although the fo'c'stle decking itself has largely rotted away and now allows views into the rooms below. Her two foredeck holds still hold their coal but are well silt filled. Sturdy cargo winches are set on the deck in between the hatches beside the stump of her foremast. Derricks lie fallen across the hatches.

The bridge superstructure is still recognisable – dotted with portholes at main deck level and the deck levels above rotted away to reveal the skeletal framework of her structure. Steps lead up from the foredeck at either side of the deckhouse – and once would have allowed passage along either side of the superstructure. Behind the bridge superstructure another cargo hatch allows access to the Hold below and separates the bridge area from the Engine Room superstructure. On top, aft of the circular funnel opening, a large rectangular hatch opens down into the roof of the engine room and allows fine views of the large triple-expansion engine with catwalks around it. Her two aft holds are still brim full of high-grade Welsh coal,

sorted in different sizes. Her broken off main mast stands in between the Hatches with cargo winches fore and aft of it. Towards the stern, her spare anchor still sits chained in place on the deck. Her rounded stern, rudder and propeller – dropping away into the blackness – are a magnificent sight.

SS THESIS, SOUND OF MULL

The wreck of the small, delicate 19th-century iron steamship *Thesis* provides a complete contrast to the robust 20th-century Sound of Mull wrecks such as the *Hispania* and *Shuna*. She is a glimpse of an earlier generation of steamship – constructed to different principles and design.

The 151-nt *Thesis* was built in Belfast by McIlwaine, Lewis & Co., Engineers & Iron Ship Builders, and was launched in January 1887. She measured just 167 ft in length – only slightly larger than the deep-sea steam trawlers of the 20th century. She had a delicate beam of just 25 ft and a draft of 11.7 ft. She was simply constructed, her weather deck being set with three large hatches to cargo holds below, ranged fore and aft of a small midships superstructure, which held her bridge, boiler and engine room.

In October 1889, just a little over two years after her launch, the *Thesis* set out on a voyage from Middlesbrough to Belfast with a crew of 11, under the command of a Captain Wallace. Her holds were full with a cargo of pig iron, destined for the thriving shipyards in Belfast. She steamed up the east coast of Britain, past Edinburgh and Aberdeen, before crossing the Moray Firth and then rounding the very northern tip of the mainland at John O'Groats. She passed west along the notorious Pentland Firth and then as she passed Cape Wrath on her port beam, she swung her bows to head south down the west coast towards Skye. From here, her route would take her south past the islands of Canna, Rhum, Eigg and Muck, and with Coll on her starboard beam she would enter the Sound of Mull, before running down to Islay and then making the crossing of the North Channel of the Irish Sea to Belfast.

The wreck of SS Thesis, Sound of Mull.

© Rod Macdonald

By midnight on Tuesday 15 October, the *Thesis* was well down the Sound of Mull and was approaching the southernmost exit into the Firth of Lorne – which can be a difficult channel to navigate at night. The unlit rocks of Sgeir nan Gobhar clutter the south side of the Sound, and not far to the north, almost in the middle of the entrance, the small rocky islands and drying islets of Glass Eileanan guard the south side of the entrance to the Sound. The main shipping channel here is less than half a mile wide and passes between the Glass Eileanan rocks to the south and the larger rocky islets of Eilean Rubha an Ridire off the north shore of the Sound in Inninmore Bay.

Suddenly, in the pitch darkness of the autumn night, the *Thesis* shuddered as she ran onto Eilean Rubha an Ridire on the north side of the Sound at Inninmore Point. She was badly holed and it quickly became clear that the ship was doomed. The lifeboats were lowered and the crew abandoned ship, rowing safely to the nearby shore. Just a few hours after striking the reef, the *Thesis* slipped beneath the surface of the Sound of Mull and settled in her final resting place, in 100 feet of water.

The wreck now sits upright on her keel, her bows pointing to the rugged rocks of Eilean Rubha an Ridire, less than 100 metres away. She sits on a sand and boulder seabed that slopes off into the depths – her bows resting in 20 metres and her stern in 32 metres.

Her hull is largely intact, although near the bow she is missing some plates that were removed in the 1970s. The iron plates, made before *Enola Gay* ushered in the nuclear age at Hiroshima on 6 August 1945, now have a very particular use. The manufacture of steel involves a lot of air being drawn in, and thus the usual ambient radiation levels in the air tend to be concentrated and increased; Pre-Hiroshima steel – such as with all shipwrecks built before World War II – has lower levels of radiation in comparison to modern steel, and has been required for the manufacture of sensitive medical radiation monitors. (Similar plating has also been removed from some of the German World War I wrecks at Scapa Flow, and from HMS *Port Napier*, off Skye.)

Open hatches and the skeletal framework of her ribs near the bow allow easy access into her foredeck holds – all her holds are now empty, having been divested of their cargo of pig iron long ago. The central midships superstructure was most probably constructed of wood on a metal frame – but it has completely rotted away to leave the large boiler and engine now sitting half exposed above the main weather deck.

Aft of her engine room the stump of her main mast sits on the deck with cargo winches beside it. The hatch to her after deck hold allows access below decks and a further hatch marks where her poop accommodation was situated. Delicate anchors still sit on the deck, one near the bows and one at the stern on the port side.

Shipwreck – the essentials	
Type of wreck	steamship
Nationality	British
Launched	January 1887
Dimensions	167 ft x 25 ft x 11.7 ft
Tonnage	151nt
Date sunk	15 October 1889
Cause of sinking	running onto rocks at Inninmore Point
Depth of water	32 metres
Least depth above wreck	18 metres
Position	56° 29.920N, 005° 41.504W

SS *HISPANIA*, SOUND OF MULL

In the days before Christmas 1954, somber headlines in national newspapers focused attention on another shipping loss in the Sound of Mull: 'Swedish steamer sinks in the Sound of Mull, captain goes down with his ship'.

Above left: Main mast H frame and cargo winches between the aft holds, SS Hispania © Ewan Rowell

Above right: Raised companionway doorway at the bow of the SS Hispania © Ewan Rowell

Above right: Anchor chain and windlass at the bow of the SS Hispania © *Ewan Rowell*

Above: Auxiliary steering gear at the stern of the SS Hispania © *Ewan Rowell*

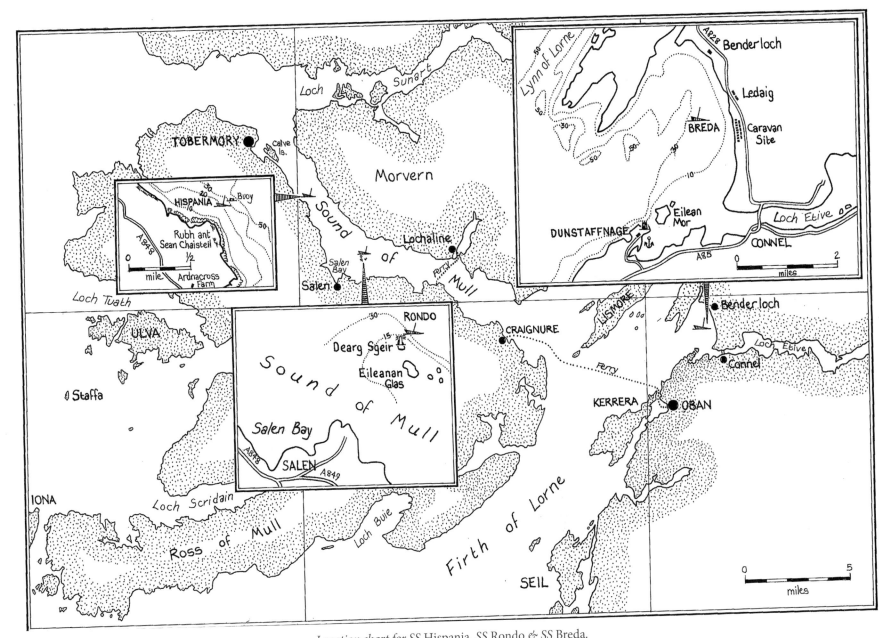

Location chart for SS Hispania, SS Rondo & SS Breda.

Right: Deep in the engine room of the SS Hispania © Ewan Rowell

Far right: SS Hispania.

Below: The wreck of the SS Hispania in the Sound of Mull.

© Rod Macdonald

The *Hispania*, a veteran old lady of the seas built more than 40 years earlier in 1912 on the River Schelde in Belgium, had run onto the Sgeir More (Gaelic for 'Big Rock') in the treacherous narrow Sound of Mull.

The *Hispania* had set out on 17 December 1954 on a voyage from Liverpool to Varberg, near Gothenburg in Sweden, with a cargo of steel, asbestos and sheet rubber. From the Liverpool docks, she steamed north through the Irish Sea and passed through the North Channel – the narrow bottleneck that separates Ireland from Scotland. She moved into the exposed Atlantic, and into a fierce westerly Atlantic winter storm.

As she moved up the west coast of Scotland, the 57-year-old Captain Ivor Dahn, who hailed from Gothenburg, sought protection from the storm by using the west coast islands and coastline wherever he could. On the evening of Saturday 18 December, *Hispania* rounded the Ross of Mull and passed by Duart Castle on its port side as she entered the treacherous Sound of Mull. Here in the Sound, flanked by land on both sides, it was hoped there would be some protection from the weather.

In the near zero visibility of the storm and with little forgiving space in the Sound, at about 9 p.m., in the blackness of a December night a navigational error lured the *Hispania* onto the Sgeir Mhor: the large rock situated just a few hundred metres off the mainland shore of the Sound, beside Glenmorven Cottage. Its top lies completely submerged just two or three metres beneath the surface most of the time, but at low water dries out by just 1.2 metres. To the shock of her crew and Captain Dahn, the *Hispania* suddenly ground to a shuddering halt. Captain Dahn ordered her engines astern, but as she came off Sgeir Mhor and moved back out into the Sound, she immediately started listing to port. It became clear very quickly that she was going to sink.

There was no panic aboard. The crew below decks who had turned in earlier had time to get dressed and the lifeboats were lowered. As the crew boarded the boats, Captain Dahn refused to leave his ship. The storm had by this time abated and for an hour the crew in the lifeboats rowed round the stricken vessel, shouting and pleading with their captain to board one of the boats. Captain Dahn steadfastly refused as his vessel sank deeper and deeper into the water. Suddenly, with the weight of water inside her, an internal bulkhead gave way and *Hispania* gave a lurch. The remainder of her hull flooded quickly and she soon disappeared from sight, having drifted across the Sound until she was less than half a mile off the coast of Mull. Captain Dahn was last seen standing in the bridge as the ship went under, with his hand to his forehead in a salute. Once *Hispania* had disappeared, the crew rowed to the shore. Captain Dahn's body was never found.

The crew rowed both lifeboats for 45 minutes to the mainland shore, landing about half a mile from Glenmorven Cottage. Here, locals rallied to their plight offering typical Highland hospitality and assistance. The 21-man crew were driven in local cars to the nearby slip at the small village of Drimnin, just a mile or two to the north, where a launch coming down from Tobermory, on Mull, would pick them up. The crew were cold and exhausted, but on hearing of their plight, the local Drimnin postmistress, Mrs. Cameron, sent word down to the slip that she would have something made for them. In small groups the crew came up to her house, where they were given tea and something to eat. Speaking later about the incident she recalled: "It was a job feeding 21 men without warning, but fortunately, being so far away from the shops, we always have a good stock of food in hand, so I managed quite well."

At about 2 a.m., early on Sunday, the launch *Lochbuie* hove to as near the tiny slip at Drimnin as it could. The local ferryman and Mrs. Cameron's son ferried the seamen out to the launch. The crew were then taken to Tobermory, where the Lloyd's agent had arranged for them to get a hot meal and a bed in the Mishnish Hotel. Later in the day, they were taken across to Oban on the mainland. Some of the crew were still dressed in their boiler suits and rubber boots, so some local Oban shop-keepers opened up their shops – even though it was the Sabbath – and new clothes were given to the men before their journey back to Sweden.

Today the *Hispania* makes a fantastic wreck dive for all levels of diver. The Sound of Mull's visibility is renowned throughout the UK, and in the area of the *Hispania* it averages 10–20 metres and allows divers to see large sections of this neat, tidy and compact steamship at any one time.

The ship still sits on her keel on a sloping rocky seabed with a pronounced and increasing list to her starboard side. She is structurally intact and still carries some of her cargo in her holds. At her bow her anchor chains still are held secure on the deck as they run to her chain locker. An aft facing raised companionway doorway allowed access below to storerooms. Her foremast, which stood proudly until just a few years ago, has fallen to her starboard side. Her two foredeck cargo hatches are open allowing an easy exploration down to her cargo.

Her bridge superstructure is still impressive – a skeletal latticework of struts and spars with the captain's bath still in place in his quarters on the starboard side. Aft of the bridge, and just aft of the funnel opening, the pitched roof of her engine allows views and access down into the engine room.

Her sturdy main mast still stands in between her two after deck cargo hatches and towards her stern, and just in front of the poop deck superstructure, her spare propeller sits neatly stored in a small hold. At the very stern is the T-shaped auxiliary steering column for direct turning of the rudder below. The wreck sits on an underwater shelf, and not far away from the stern the shelf drops off in to the deep blackness of the middle of the Sound.

The Rondo *stranded on the rocky island of Dearg Sgeir soon after running aground. She is still making smoke and one of her lifeboats is partially lowered from it davits.*

SS *RONDO*, SOUND OF MULL

The 2,363-ton dry cargo standard ship, *Rondo*, was built in Tampa, Florida in 1917, ostensibly for the Cunard Steamship Co. – but in reality for the British war effort. During the early years of World War I, German U-boats had taken a heavy toll on British shipping. By the end of 1915 alone, some 1,600,000 tons of British shipping had been sunk, and hard-pressed British shipyards were unable to build enough new ships to replace the losses. In its time of need, the British Government turned to the neutral American ship-building industry for assistance.

In America, old ailing shipyards were updated and enlarged - and scores of brand new shipyards were set up. By March 1917, orders to US yards for new British ships amounted to almost three-quarters of a million tons. These ships were to be mass-produced to simplified 'standard' designs – with standard hulls and engines. These 'standard' ships were all given a standard nomenclature with the word *War* being prefixed to their names. At the time of her construction, the *Rondo* was called *War Wonder (I)*.

Shipwreck – the essentials	
Type of wreck	steamship
Nationality	Swedish
Launched	1912
Dimensions	236.8 ft x 37.3 ft x 16.2 ft
Tonnage	1,377 grt
Date sunk	18 December 1954
Cause of sinking	striking the Sgeir Mhor rocks.
Depth of water	30 metres
Least depth above wreck	20 metres
Position	56° 34.93N, 005° 59.22W

Above: Stern view of the Rondo *inclined down towards the underwater cliff of Dearg Sgeir.*

Left: The rocky islet of Dearg Sgeir. The buoy in the foreground is tied to the uppermost rudder post of the Rondo.

When America herself entered the war, on 6 April 1917, as part of their own war effort they immediately requisitioned all merchant vessels then under construction in US yards. Some 400 hulls were swiftly transferred to US Government ownership and *War Wonder (I)* (still under construction) was one of the requisitioned ships. Once requisitioned, the US Government renamed her *Lithopolis*. She was completed late in the war, in September 1918 – only two months before the Armistice of November 1918 halted the hostilities.

In all, some 3,500 'tramp' ships had been constructed, but after the war, the pressing need for vast numbers of such ships was gone – they were suddenly surplus to requirements. Some were broken up; others were laid up in rivers

until they found use again in World War II. The Ford Motor Co. purchased a batch of 200 tramp ships to be scrapped in Detroit and re-used as automobiles.

The *Lithopolis* escaped such a fate: instead, the US Government sold her off to a private shipping company and she went to work on the seas. In 1930, after a change of ownership she was renamed *Laurie*, and finally in 1934, she was taken into Norwegian ownership and renamed *Rondo*.

In January 1935, she set off in ballast from the Clyde to pass round the north of Scotland on her way down to Dunstan, in Northumberland, to pick up a cargo bound for Oslo.

On 25 January, as she travelled up the west coast of Scotland on the first leg of her voyage, she halted her journey in Aros Bay, near Tobermory, at the north end of the Sound of Mull, to seek shelter from a raging blizzard. Just after 9 p.m., that evening, in the face of a furious wind her anchor chain parted and she drifted powerless down the narrow Sound in pitch darkness – for almost seven miles. Eventually, she ran aground on a shallow reef running out from the tiny rocky outcrop known as Dearg Sgeir, right beside its distinctive small white navigation beacon. There is still a light on the little island to this day – an essential guide to night navigation in the Sound.

Over the coming weeks, trawlers, a tug from Greenock and a salvage vessel from Southampton all made successive attempts to haul her off the rocks. But all these attempts failed and eventually her insurers declared her a total loss and ordered that she be broken down for scrap. In the weeks and months thereafter, she was scrapped *in situ* on the reef.

The salvage crew initially lived aboard her whilst they worked, but as they stripped her down they lost their accommodation. They then set up camp on the small island, working aboard her by day and camping beside her at night. The crew managed to cut the *Rondo* almost down to her waterline, but before the job was completed, heavy seas drove *Rondo*'s skeletal remains off the reef. She plunged down the near vertical underwater cliffs of the islet, until her bows ploughed into the seabed 50 metres below.

Today, almost 80 years later, the *Rondo* still stands in this unnatural and seemingly precarious position – a unique spectacle in British diving. Her

The **Rondo**.

© Rod Macdonald

uppermost rudder is only 3 metres beneath the surface whilst her bows are well buried in the seabed in 50 metres of water, with only a few inches now protruding above the sandy bottom. She is rightly regarded as one of the greatest wreck dives in Scottish waters, although it is disconcerting to be floating beside a ship standing vertically on her bow: a ship that disappears straight down into the darkness below.

Her keel and hull up to her old waterline is fairly intact and offers protection inside the open space from the current. Divers can follow the propeller shaft down to where it meets the engine room. The H-frame of the mainmast and a section of the original hull and weather deck around it (not cut away during the salvage works) are still upright and jut out an angle from the rest of the stripped-down hull.

Passing deeper beyond the mainmast, the hull is filled with a jumble of machinery and plating, but then beyond 35 metres and as the seabed approaches, the incline of the wreck starts to flatten out. The hull becomes an empty void as you near the stem of the bow, buried deep in the seabed. Turning here to ascend, with eyes now dark-adjusted, divers can see the silhouette of this fine wreck towering above them, and leading the way back up to the light of the surface.

Shipwreck – the essentials

Type of wreck	dry cargo ship
Nationality	Norwegian
Launched	September 1918
Dimensions	264 ft x 42 ft x 21.2 ft
Tonnage	3,500 dwt; 2,363 grt
Date sunk	25 January 1935
Cause of sinking	running aground on Dearg Sgeir
Depth of water	50 metres
Least depth above wreck	3 metres
Position	56° 32.165N, 005° 54.40W

SS *BREDA*, OBAN

The 6,941-grt steamship *Breda* is perhaps one of Scotland's most famous and popular wrecks – a wreck that is visited by most UK divers at some stage of their career. She sits upright on an even keel in a sheltered bay near Oban. She is a big, structurally virtually intact ship, lying in relatively shallow shelving water of 30 metres at most. The least depth down to her main deck is about15 metres so she is an ideal wreck dive both for the novice, but also for the experienced diver.

The *Breda* was a large and beautiful steamship some 402.6 ft in length, with a beam of 58.3 ft and a draft of 34.7 ft. She was built in 1921 by the New Waterway Shipbuilding Co. at Schiedam, just south of Rotterdam, in Holland. She had three decks, a cruiser stern and a flat bottom – but her most distinctive features were two large goalpost masts; one forward and one aft of the main central superstructure.

For nearly 20 years following her construction, she plied the seas carrying large cargoes across the stormy waters between Europe and South America. Her service speed was 11.8 knots and she proved to be a seaworthy and safe ship.

Stern view of the SS Breda.

When World War II erupted over Europe in 1939, the *Breda* – although a Dutch cargo vessel – was under the control of the British P&O Line. A defensive (DEMS) gun-platform was mounted on top of her stern accommodation superstructure.

The *Breda* set out for Oban from London on 12 December 1940 scheduled for a voyage from there on a circuitous route that would eventually take her to Mombasa, Bombay and on to Karachi. She reached Oban on 20 December and took up a holding position in the Oban Roads to await orders to form up in convoy. The Oban Roads is one of the deepest stretches of sheltered water around Britain's shores and had been chosen as a convoy gathering point because its great depth made it safe from any enemy attempts to lay mines. Several other merchant ships were anchored nearby.

The wreck of SS Breda, *by Oban.*

In her cavernous holds she carried a general mixed cargo of 3,000 tons of cement, 175 tons of tobacco and cigarettes, three Hawker biplanes, 30 De Havilland Moths aircraft and spares, military lorry spares, NAAFI crockery, copper ingots, nine dogs and ten horses rumoured to belong to the Aga Khan.

After the German occupation of Norway in April 1940, the Nazis had gained control of Norwegian air bases and started to launch bombing raids against shipping, industry and cities across Scotland and northern England.

Six months after the occupation of Norway, just before 3 p.m. on 23 December 1940, a small group of German Heinkel 111 bombers lifted slowly into the air from their Norwegian air base, heavily laden with bombs. Their distinctive glazed nose cones gave the pilot and navigator unrivalled all-round visibility. The bombers laboured into the air and slowly took 20 minutes to climb to the maximum height they could achieve with this payload – 16,400 feet. Each Heinkel carried four 551-lb bombs nose up in its bomb bay, and two larger 1,102-lb bombs on outside tracks. At their fully laden speed of 193 mph, they would take just under three hours to reach their target for the day – the Oban Roads.

The Heinkel's were the most vulnerable of the Luftwaffe's bombers – they were relatively slow and unmanoeuvrable and would be easy prey for any fast RAF fighters that intercepted them. Since the end of the Battle of Britain a few months before – where their shortcomings had been realised – Heinkel's had been largely confined to a night-bombing role. By the end of 1940, only a few daring daylight raids were being made against the British mainland – but it would be one such raid that would send the *Breda* to the bottom.

Suddenly, at 5.45 p.m., the crew of the *Breda* heard the unfamiliar drone of German aircraft as the flight of Heinkel's flashed in at speed on their bombing run. The ships at anchor were taken completely by surprise, the attack being so swift that no air-raid siren was set off and the crews did not have time to man their anti-aircraft guns to fight back. They were sitting ducks.

From the multitude of virtually defenceless ships anchored below, one Heinkel picked out the large silhouette of the *Breda* as its target and started its bomb run. A stick of four 551-lb bombs was loosed by the bomb-aimer, apparently directly on target. However, the bombs straddled the *Breda*, missing a direct hit but exploding in the water close beside the ship with such force that the whole vessel shook. The blasts fractured internal piping and sheared off a cooling water inlet pipe in the engine room. Seawater started to flood into the engine room, and within a few minutes the water had killed all steam and stopped the ship's electrics.

The *Breda* was now without power – and dead in the water as she flooded. She started to sink steadily by the stern and developed a list to starboard. With all their bombs dropped, the Heinkel's turned and fled back towards Norway as fast as they could – before RAF fighters could be scrambled to mount a pursuit.

At 6 p.m., the lifeboats were lowered and the *Breda*'s passengers were boarded and safely rowed to the shore.

At 6.15 p.m., an Admiralty tug came alongside and took the *Breda* in tow, heading towards the shallower water of Ardmucknish Bay, where it was hoped she could be beached and saved. After being towed for two hours, at 8.10 p.m., the tug maneuvered *Breda* over a 6-metre-deep shelf and let go of the tow-cable. The *Breda*, heavy and low in the water, lost her momentum and came to a shuddering standstill, beaching her bow on the edge of the shelf. The horses were released into the water and allowed to swim ashore (the last survivor of the Aga Khan's horses is said to have lived to a ripe old age and died near Oban in 1967). At 8.30 p.m., the captain – the last man aboard – clambered down into a lifeboat and was rowed ashore.

With the coming of the following day, it was felt that the ship was salvageable and work started immediately. But only a fraction of the cargo had been taken off, when the *Breda*, pounded by winter seas and pulled by the tide, slid off the shelf and slewed down the sloping seabed into deeper water.

In 1943, some small-scale salvage works were carried out and salvage divers recovered some copper ingots. Thereafter, the wreck was left in peace: marked by her goal post masts, which showed at low water.

In 1961, at the request of the Northern Lighthouse Board, the Royal Navy swept her with wire to a depth of 28 feet, removed her rotted bridge and her fo'c'stle and brought down her masts. Now completely hidden from sight, memory of her passed.

In 1966, sport divers from the Edinburgh branch of the BSAC (British Sub Aqua Club) rediscovered her. Legend has it that the first sport dive on the *Breda* was made by a solitary diver who snorkeled out for almost a mile from the shore, before descending to find a largely intact shipwreck, its holds still full of its wartime cargo. In the late 1960s, local divers carried out some other salvage work and the propeller was successfully dug out from its tomb of silt, blasted off and lifted.

Today, the wreck of the *Breda* is a classic UK dive. Her hull is still structurally intact and, as she sits on an even keel, her layout is easy to understand. Her very size is dominating and she is a large vessel to circumnavigate. At her bow, there is an obvious scar where her fo'c'stle was cut away and removed by the Royal Navy in 1961 – it lies on the seabed not far away. Her vast cavernous foredeck holds are black ominous

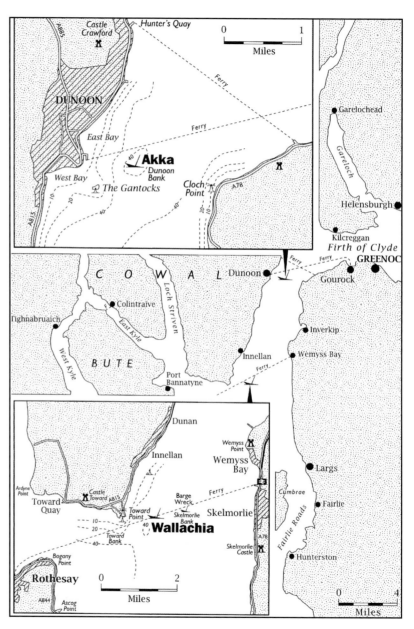

Location chart for MV Akka & SS Wallachia.

Shipwreck – the essentials

Type of wreck	steamship
Nationality	Dutch
Launched	1921
Dimensions	402.6 ft x 58.3 ft x 34.7 ft
Tonnage	6,941 grt
Date sunk	23 December 1940
Cause of sinking	bombed by Heinkel 111
Depth of water	30 metres
Least depth above wreck	15 metres
Position	56° 28.33N, 005° 25.00W

places to drop into, but still hold much of her wartime cargo. The rotted skeleton of some of her bridge superstructure remains – with a cargo hatch separating it from the engine room superstructure. Two further aft holds are filled with cargo – in one hold, stacked bags of concrete now set hard form an impenetrable wall. At her stern stands another poop superstructure with the remains of the DEMS defensive gun emplacement on top.

There is no appreciable current to worry about and she can be dived at most states of the tide. Her relatively shallow depth makes her ideal for all types of divers and allows long-duration dives.

MV AKKA, FIRTH OF CLYDE

The huge 5,409-grt wreck of the Swedish motor vessel *Akka* is the largest diveable wreck in the Firth of Clyde today. Being a relatively recent wreck from the 1950's, she is largely intact and divers can swim along corridors and through cabins, and drift from one deck-level to the next. Lying in a barren mud desert, the wreck has become an artificial reef, populated by huge shoals of fish, her steel work covered in soft corals, dead men's fingers and a blaze of orange and plumrose anemones.

The *Akka* was built in Gothenburg, Sweden and launched in July 1942. She measured 442 ft 10 in. length, with a beam of 56 ft and a draft of just over 25 ft. She had a service speed of 12.5 knots. Most of her length below decks was given over to cavernous cargo holds – she had eight 26-ft-wide deck hatches allowing access to them.

Her main superstructure was located midships and extended aft above

© Rod Macdonald

Top: The wreck of the MV Akka, *Firth of Clyde.*

Above: MV Akka *in her wartime colours.*

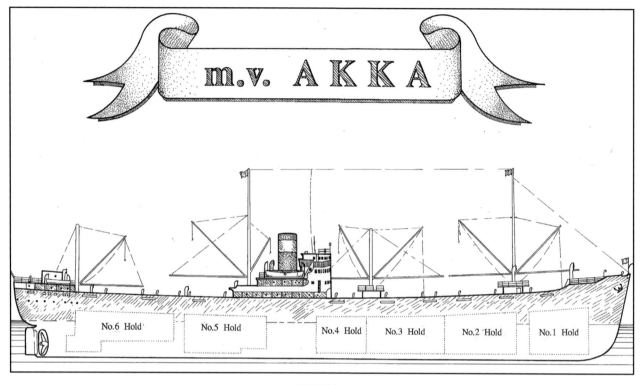

MV Akka.

rounded the Mull of Kintyre and entered the Firth of Clyde – journey's end was close at hand. Continuing up the Firth, she passed the Isle of Arran on her port side and at 8.15 p.m., she passed Small Cumbrae Light.

At 9.22 p.m., the captain ordered the vessel to slow to half-speed, to take on a local pilot, and then ordered a change of course to avoid the notorious Gantock Rocks: a dangerous clump of rocks that rise up from the depths to break the surface about a mile off the coast beside Dunoon. A small tower with an unmanned light flashes a warning of their dangerous location to mariners.

After the order to change course was given, the captain noticed that the *Akka* was responding very slowly to her rudder. All the while, the Gantock Rocks were growing ever larger in front of him. Unable to steer his ship away from the Gantocks, he ordered the engines stopped – but the forward momentum of her 5,409 tons was too much and she carried onto the Gantocks. Residents ashore in nearby Dunoon and in Gourock on the other side of the Clyde, heard the awful sound of her hull grinding onto the rock and being torn open to the sea. Concerned townsfolk started to gather ashore, helpless as the drama unfolded before them.

The Gantocks had torn the *Akka*'s hull open along almost half her length, from Hold No 2 aft. With each passing second, tons of water was flooding

the engine room, housing the hospital, crew's mess, galley and the engineers' quarters. The promenade deck area held the lounge, saloon and officers' cabins. On the boat deck above, the captain's cabin and dayroom could be found with nearby lifeboats hanging in their davits. Above the captain's accommodation was the navigating bridge deck, which housed the wheelhouse and radio room. At her very stern, a large deckhouse held the crew's cabins, and above this was the crew's bar. After a sea-career of just 14 years, disaster struck the *Akka*, in the River Clyde as she approached Glasgow.

On Wednesday, 4 April 1956, she had left Sweden, her holds full of a cargo of iron ore bound for Glasgow. Five days later, on Monday 9 April, the *Akka*

into the ship. The captain ordered her engines be put astern, to see if she would come off the rocks so that perhaps he could save her by beaching her on the nearby shore. She slid off the rocks – but as she did so, the rate of water rushing into her increased. It became clear that she was lost.

The order to abandon ship was given and the lifeboats were lowered from the midships superstructure, and from above the crew's accommodation deckhouse at the very stern.

Just 3–4 minutes after running aground, the *Akka* heeled over onto her port side and sank quickly. As the cold water made contact with her boilers there was a loud explosion.

The *Akka* went down so quickly that some of the lifeboats had not been rowed far enough away to escape the suction when she made her final plunge. A number of the lifeboats were sunk and their unfortunate occupants pitched into the water. Thankfully, many people ashore had witnessed the stranding, and within minutes, a number of rescue vessels had arrived at the scene and started picking up survivors. Twenty-seven of the crew were saved and three lost. Sadly, three of the survivors also later died.

The *Akka* righted herself as she sank to the bottom – landing on an even keel on the seabed. The topmost 12 feet of her masts projected up above the surface – marking her position but posing a significant danger for shipping. Three months later, a passing fishing vessel hit the masts and this prompted action to be taken. In September 1956, divers from Metal Industries, (the famous salvers who worked the scuttled German WWI Fleet in Scapa Flow) used explosives to blast off the top two deck levels at the front of her bridge superstructure, along with her funnel and masts. The latter lie on the wreck where they fell.

Today, the massive wreck of the *Akka* sits on an even keel on a sloping bottom. Her bows rest in 30 metres and her stern in 40 metres. Her hull is still structurally intact, but her superstructures are now well decayed and collapsing. Fixed stairs lead down on either side of her raised foc'stle to her main deck where set in between the foremost of her holds the stump of her foremast can be found, the mast fallen to lie over the cargo hatches behind. Some of the mechanized covers on runners for her ore-holds remain closed –

others are withdrawn, leaving the holds open: massive black voids dropping down into the depths. Just in front of her bridge superstructure the cut off remains of two king posts can be found with winches dotted around them.

The two remaining deck levels of the bridge superstructure hold much of interest for the diver and the salvage works have made access to the engine room relatively easy. Aft of the superstructure more cargo holds, with their covers still in place can be found. The sizeable aftcastle has a companionway walkway ringing completely around the graceful curving stern. And just forward the cut down remains of her aft kingposts can be spotted.

Shipwreck – the essentials	
Type of wreck	motor vessel – ore carrier
Nationality	Swedish
Launched	July 1942
Dimensions	442 ft 10 in. x 56 ft 9 in. x 25 ft 11 in.
Tonnage	5,409 grt
Date sunk	9 April 1956
Cause of sinking	grounding on the Gantock Rocks
Depth of water	30–40 metres
Least depth above wreck	16 metres
Position	55° 56.43N, 004° 54.20W

SS *WALLACHIA*, FIRTH OF CLYDE

Almost 60 years after his death, Sir William Burrell (1861–1958) is still a household name in Scotland, forever associated with the Burrell Art Collection he gifted to the city of Glasgow, now housed in a fine gallery at Pollock Park. Most will have heard of the Burrell Collection, but few know that a small part of the shipping empire that created his vast wealth lies silent and still, not far away in the dark depths of the Clyde: the beautiful and graceful steamship, SS *Wallachia*.

The 1,724-grt *Wallachia* was built in Southampton and launched in March 1883. She was a small, sleek vessel, just 259.2 ft long with a beam of 36.1 ft. Once launched, she was put to work on the Black Sea run before being sold to the Glasgow shipping line William Burrell & Son. She then started plying Burrell's well-worn passage from Glasgow to the Empire colonies of the West Indies.

In September 1895, the *Wallachia* was scheduled for another run out to the West Indies. As she lay berthed at Glasgow Queen's Dock, her holds were carefully filled with coal, gin, whisky, beer, building materials, books, stationery, glassware, earthenware and other general goods – all designed to ease the rigours of life in the West Indies.

At 10 a.m., on 29 September 1895, her mooring ropes were cast off, and with a crew of 21 and one solitary passenger, she headed out into the River Clyde on the first leg of her voyage across the Atlantic.

Conditions on the river were poor. A heavy fog hung in the air – so thick that just two hours into her journey, she had to halt off the Tail of the Bank near Greenock to wait for visibility to improve.

In the early afternoon, the fog lifted slightly – enough to let her get under way again. Her engine was put ahead and her single-screw churned the water at her stern as she gathered way and headed further down the river.

Just before 4 p.m., she entered a thicker bank of fog and in the poor visibility she ran aground on a shoal off Innellan Pier, near the southmost point of the Cowal Peninsula. Luckily, the tide was rising and she quickly refloated and was able to continue her journey.

At 4.10 p.m., however, about a mile east of Toward Point, her luck ran out when the bows of the 1,406-grt Norwegian steamship *Flos*, suddenly loomed out of the fog, bearing down hard and close on her starboard bow. There was no time for the *Wallachia* to react to the danger – the captain managed to order: "All hands clear of the fo'c'stle!" just before the bows of the *Flos* rammed the *Wallachia*'s starboard bow. With the momentum of her 1,406 tons behind her, the *Flos*'s sheer bow effortlessly sliced through the *Wallachia*'s more vulnerable iron hull plates.

The captain of the *Flos* initially kept his engines ahead in order to keep the two vessels locked together, and the order to abandon ship was given. The *Wallachia*'s four lifeboats were lowered – the first capsizing as it was lowered in the confusion. The crew managed to safely board two of the remaining three lifeboats and started to row towards the shore.

Once the *Wallachia*'s crew was safely clear of the ship, the captain of the *Flos* decided to attempt to take the *Wallachia* in tow to shallower water, to see if she could be grounded and saved. But, as he put her engines astern and reversed away, he unplugged the gash in the *Wallachia*'s side. The rate of water flooding into her hull increased dramatically and she immediately began to settle quickly by the bow. The attempt to take her in tow was abandoned.

At about 4.35 p.m. – just 25 minutes after the collision – the *Wallachia* went down by the bows. As cold seawater made contact with her boilers there was a large explosion. She sank into 35 metres of water, landing upright on her keel on the seabed.

Once the *Wallachia* was on the bottom and the dark waters of the Clyde had closed over her, she was soon forgotten about and her memory passed into oblivion. Her wreck was last marked on an Admiralty Chart in 1905, but that mark disappeared from subsequent charts. She was lost to the world for 80 years, until her rediscovery for sport diving in 1977, by the Girvan branch of the Scottish Sub Aqua Club.

Today, the wreck of the *Wallachia* is one of the most loved and most dived wrecks in the Clyde. Her fine lines are so distinctive of 19th century steamships: she is a relic of a bygone age; a tantalising glimpse of the majestic days of steam.

One of her holds – some 20 ft square and 20 ft deep – is still filled to just a few feet from its top with thousands of distinctive dark green/brown beer bottles, most still with their contents and corks intact. The bottles come in four sizes: larger pale ale bottles about a foot high and smaller bottles for stout. Many of the corks still clearly bear the words 'McEwan's Edinburgh'

The wreck of the SS Wallachia, lost in the Clyde in 1895 on a voyage to the West Indies.

along their sides and look as fresh as the day they were put in. The beer in them, although no longer drinkable, smells exactly the same as today's McEwan's Export – one of the top-selling beers in the UK to this day and still known in the export market as McEwan's India Pale Ale.

The gash on the starboard side of her bows, where the *Flos* rammed her, is so large that a diver can swim through it. The foredeck holds are silt-filled, but still hold much of their original cargo. The midships bridge superstructure is still relatively intact, with its forward-looking portholes and entry doors either side. The roof has rotted away completely, allowing easy entry and exit.

Immediately behind the bridge are the captain's quarters. Aft of that is the 6 ft. wide black hole of the funnel, its steel long ago rotted completely away. Divers can drop down the funnel hole into the engine room, where the engine itself still sits on the centre-line of the ship with catwalks along either side. Above, the distinctive sky-lights of a classic engine room pitched roof – the glass long gone – still allow weak ambient light from the surface to illuminate the darkness.

There are two main aft holds astern of the superstructure. Hold No 3 is well filled with silt, but Hold No 4 – the beer hold – is an amazing sight.

Shipwreck – the essentials

Type of wreck	steamship
Nationality	British
Launched	March 1883
Dimensions	259.2 ft x 36.1 ft x 18 ft
Tonnage	1,724 grt
Date sunk	29 September 1895
Cause of sinking	rammed by SS *Flos* in fog
Depth of water	34 metres
Least depth above wreck	25 metres
Position	55° 51.41N, 004° 57.07W

As far as a diver's torch-beam can carry in every direction, are hundreds – if not thousands – of beer bottles poking out of the silt. These bottles are stacked up from the bottom of the hold some 20 feet below: a vast total. A small hatch allows access down into the smaller aftmost Hold No 5, which although deeply filled with silt, held until recently whisky bottles with their seals intact.

HMS *PORT NAPIER*, LOCHALSH, SKYE

The wreck of HMS *Port Napier* lies in 20 metres of water in Lochalsh, the narrow stretch of sea that separates the Isle of Skye, off the west coast, from mainland Scotland. She lies only 300 metres or so from the shores of Skye, on her starboard side, and with a beam of 22 metres, at most states of the tide (except High Water), the whole of her uppermost port side stands proud of the water. She is for divers, perhaps the perfect wreck. She is largely intact, lies in shallow water and holds much of interest.

The 9,600-grt *Port Napier* had only a very short career at sea before she met her demise. She was built in 1940 in Wallsend-on-Tyne for the Port Line by Swan Hunter & Wigham Richardson Ltd. Just a few months after her launch she would be on the bottom.

The *Port Napier* was a substantial vessel: 498 ft long with a beam of 68 ft, her internal spaces given over to massive cargo holds. She was launched on 23 April 1940, but due to her fast design speed of 16.5 knots and huge cargo carrying capability, on 12 June 1940, whilst she was still being fitted out afloat, she was requisitioned by the Ministry of War Transport and immediately converted to a mine-layer.

Her original peacetime design was heavily modified following her requisition to meet the Admiralty's needs as a mine-layer. The hatches to her holds were completely decked over, save for a small mine-loading hatch near the stern. Two 4-inch guns were mounted on the foredeck near her bow, four 20-mm anti-aircraft guns mounted amidships, and additionally, she was fitted out with two 2-pounder anti-aircraft guns and two 5-inch anti-aircraft guns.

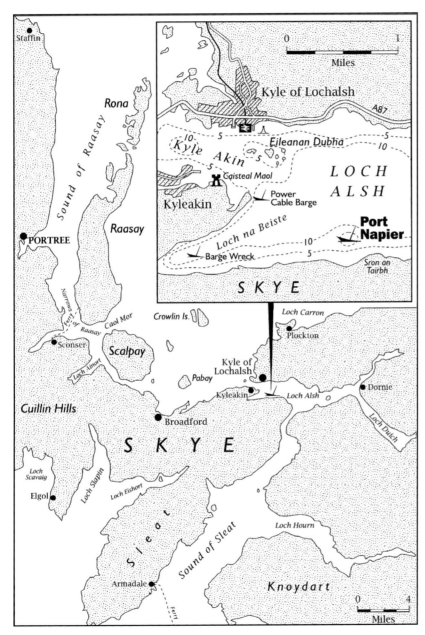

Location chart for HMS Port Napier.

She was designed to carry a payload of 550 contact-mines on trolleys. To allow these to be deployed, four mine-laying doors were cut into the curve of her stern, and narrow gauge railways were laid internally from each stern door along corridors that led to the holds – where her cargo of mines was stored. Each mine was attached by a chain to its own rail-trolley. When the mines were being deployed, the trolley with the chained mine sitting on top was pushed from the hold, along the railway corridor and then pushed out through the mine-laying door at the stern. The chain would have been pre-cut to the length required for the depth of water the mines were being laid in. The trolley sank to the seabed and acted as an anchor to hold the mine as it floated upwards. Usually, mines would be deployed at a depth of about 30 feet from the surface – deep enough to allow small vessels to pass harmlessly above without detonating the valuable mine. Larger vessels would not be so lucky.

Once ready for action, *HMS Port Napier* was tasked to form part of the 1st Minelaying Squadron that operated from 1940–1943 from port 'ZA' – Scotland. The squadron was detailed to mine the western approaches to the British Isles.

After a very short service career, on 27 November 1940, *HMS Port Napier* was berthed alongside the pier at the railhead of the naval base of Kyle of Lochalsh. For days, her crew had laboured hard, carefully loading her cargo of 550 mines down through the small stern loading-hatch, and running the trolleys along the railways to storage in the holds. Her full complement of mines – all 550 – was now securely stowed below decks, along with 60,000 rounds of ammunition for her guns.

That night, the outbreak of a fire on the ship was spotted and immediate attempts were made to extinguish it. Despite this, the flames could not be controlled and started to spread through the ship. The fire got out of control and a red glow started to illuminate the night sky – it was feared that if the deadly cargo of mines went off, the town of Kyle of Lochalsh itself would be flattened. Curious locals crowded down to the docks to see what was going on, unwittingly putting themselves in great danger.

Plans were made for Kyle to be evacuated as *Port Napier* was cast off from her moorings and taken in tow away from the town. Hurried plans were also made to evacuate the residents of the small town of Kyleakin on Skye – on the other side of Lochalsh – as they now became vulnerable to any explosion, as *Port Napier* was towed closer to them.

The fires continued to get worse whilst *Port Napier* was under tow. Finally, when she had been towed to Loch no Beiste – a small, uninhabited bay about a mile or two east of Kyleakin, where the hills ashore gave some protection to the town – she was cast loose.

Shortly afterwards, there was flash that lit up the night sky momentarily, followed thereafter by a loud explosion which resonated around the nearby hills of Skye. The force of the explosion threw fragments of the ship halfway up the hills lining the shore of the bay – where they remain to this day.

Surprisingly, despite the magnitude of the explosion, none of the cargo of mines detonated. *Port Napier* rapidly filled with water, keeled over to her starboard side, and sank with her entire cargo of 550 mines and 60,000 rounds of ammunition still stacked in her holds.

In 1950, the Royal Navy decided to remove the mines to make the wreck safe. In 1955–6, a Royal Navy salvage team from HMS *Barglow* removed the entire upmost port-side plating of her hull, to expose her inner structure, decks, ribs and double bottom. Royal Navy clearance divers then rigged a lifting system to lift the mines vertically up from the holds to the surface, between each of the decks. In all, 526 mines were lifted from the wreck and 16 had to be detonated *in situ* as irrecoverable. Four-thousand of the 60,000 rounds of ammunition were also recovered. In 1998, some of her pre-Hiroshima low-radiation steel hull plates were also removed.

Today, the uppermost port-side of the hull can easily be located, standing proud of the water at most states of the tide – now blackened with age and corrosion and covered in sea life and kelp fronds. The structure of the ship is still largely intact, although internal bulkheads and plating have rotted through.

Standing on the seabed in front of her now-horizontal massive bow, is one of the highlights of diving this wreck. On her foredeck towards the bow, her two 4-inch guns still stand in their pedestal mounts above what would have been one of her foredeck holds. The foremast now juts out horizontally, defying gravity and seemingly emanating from a small deckhouse, which holds a few rooms filled with switching panels.

Her main bridge superstructure is well collapsed, and the funnel has fallen to the seabed. As divers pass towards the stern, there are numerous rotted openings, which allow glimpses into the mine-laying corridors that run almost the length of the ship. At the very stern, the four mine-laying doors are still visible, cut two above two in her stern. Experienced divers can follow the narrow gauge railways through the corridors into her massive holds. Scattered around on the seabed are a few of the mine-laying trolleys left by the Royal Navy clearance divers.

Shipwreck – the essentials	
Type of wreck	auxiliary minelayer
Nationality	British
Launched	23 April 1940
Dimensions	498 ft x 68 ft x 41.6 ft
Tonnage	9,600 grt
Date sunk	27 November 1940
Cause of sinking	fire and explosion
Depth of water	20 metres
Least depth above wreck	0 metres
Position	57° 15.58N, 005° 41.11W

Above left: HMS Port Napier.

Above: The wreck of HMS Port Napier lies in 20 metres of water 300 yards from the shores of Skye.

© Rod Macdonald

131

The wreck of MS Taurus now lies beam on to the prevailing North South currents and is slowly being covered by the shifting seabed.

5

NORTH SEA

MS *TAURUS* (III), INVERBERVIE

The motor ship, MS *Taurus (III)*, was built in 1935 in Norway, by Akers Mekaniske Verksted for the famous Wilhelmsen Line – a shipping company that started out from small beginnings in Oslo in 1864 and has continued to thrive to this day. The Wilh. Wilhelmsen Holding ASA is now a leading global maritime industry group – a massive and influential player in international shipping today.

Taurus (III) was built as a graceful fast vessel of 4,767 tons, measuring 408 ft in length, with a beam of 55 ft and boasting cavernous holds for almost her full length. She featured in *Ship of the Year* in 1935 being noted as the first Norwegian vessel to be fitted with a double acting diesel engine. The massive seven-cylinder diesel engine stood some 35 ft high and developed 4,000 bhp – enough to drive *Taurus* at a service speed of 13.5 knots: considerably faster than other steamships of older design. But for all her beauty and grace, *Taurus* would be sent to the bottom of the North Sea in 1941, just six years after her launch – one more victim of a cruel war.

After the German occupation of Norway on 9 April 1940, *Taurus* was one of the many Norwegian vessels stranded in neutral Swedish waters.

Bow shot of MS Taurus. *Courtesy of Norwegian Maritime Museum*

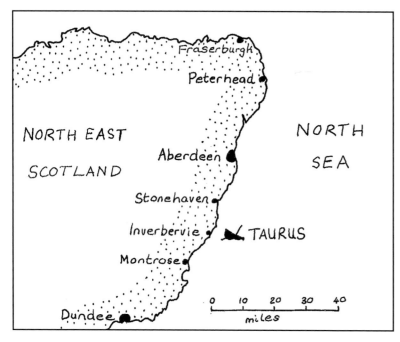

Chart showing the location of the wreck of the MS Taurus off north east Scotland.

way to the north and Denmark to the south, before breaking out into the North Sea.

The passage from Sweden to Orkney took the small flotilla 36 hours. En route, *Taurus* burnt out an exhaust valve and was stopped dead in the water for two hours whilst it was repaired. German aircraft fired on all five vessels, but none were badly damaged and they succeeded in carrying 25,000 tons of precious steel to Britain. The five ship's captains were awarded OBEs by Britain and were decorated by the King of Norway. George Binney was knighted for his daring, dangerous and brilliantly executed operation.

In May 1941, just five months after the dash from Sweden, *Taurus* was in Freetown in West Africa, completing lading a general cargo that included 2,000 tons of cocoa and 2,000 tons of groundnuts. Her routing would take her up the west coast of Africa and on to Scotland, where she would form up in the Oban Roads for a convoy. In convoy, *Taurus* would pass round the north of Scotland and then down the east coast to her eventual destination at Hull. The English Channel was simply too dangerous to risk passing through.

The voyage from Africa went uneventfully and on 5 June 1941 she was making good progress in a large convoy heading south, down the east coast of Scotland several miles offshore. Once the convoy had got in range of the German planes operating from their Norwegian airfields, continuous air attacks started up. The convoy would have to fight its way down the whole east coast of the UK.

By nightfall, as the convoy passed Aberdeen and then Stonehaven, it stretched as far as the eye could see to the north and as far again to the south. Locals still talk of helplessly watching the attacks going in from vantage points on cliffs and headlands. The night sky was lit up with the flashes of large explosions far offshore, followed some time after by the rumble.

At 00.44 a.m. on 6 June, as *Taurus* passed south of Todhead Lighthouse near Catterline, her crew heard the drone of an aircraft approaching in the darkness. Three bombs were dropped from low altitude. All three bombs missed, but like so many near misses, the force of the explosions transmitted

As a result, along with 43 of the other Wilhelmsen Line vessels stranded outside Norwegian waters, she came under the control of the Norwegian Government in exile in London – and thus under the British Ministry of War Transport.

George Binney – a British citizen working in Sweden – conceived 'Operation Rubble', in which he would use five of these stranded ships to take vital cargoes of special steel through the Skagerrak minefields, past German patrol boats, submarines and aircraft – and on to Orkney.

On 19 January 1941, at 30-minute intervals, *Taurus* and the four other ships left the small Swedish port of Brofjorden, situated to the north of Gothenburg and not far from the Norwegian border. The ships had to pass through the narrow German-controlled Skagerrak sea area, between Nor-

through the water and several of her hull plates were ruptured. She started to take on water and her engines had to be stopped. Slowly, she took on a list to port and started to settle by the stern.

A cable was passed to her from the escort trawler HMS *Tarantella* and a tow started towards the port of Montrose, some 15 miles away. The attacks on the rest of the convoy continued unabated.

Around two hours later, another aircraft attacked the stricken *Taurus*, and three more bombs were dropped. Like the last bombing run, these three bombs also narrowly missed the ship, but exploded in the water close enough to her hull for the shock to cause further damage. The rate of water flooding into her increased and she started to settle more quickly. There would be no time to tow her all the way to Montrose now.

The tow was diverted, and a desperate dash developed to drag her water-filled hulk into shallow water and beach her near the small fishing village of Johnshaven. But time had run out for *Taurus*: she sank some 2.5 miles short of safety, in 50 metres of water, her bows still pointed forlornly towards Johnshaven and the safety of the shore. She became a total loss.

The wreck settled on the bottom on an even keel, and with her bows pointed to shore, she ended up sitting broadside on to the prevailing north/south current that floods and ebbs daily up and down this coast. As the current started striking the immoveable mass of the 408-ft-long bulk of the *Taurus*, water was forced to either side and started scouring out pits underneath the bow and stern. Over a period of time, the bow and stern were eventually left suspended above their scour pits.

After almost 30 years defying gravity, held high off the seabed, the combined effects of corrosion and gravity won the battle and in 1969 the bow and stern cracked off the main body of the hull and rolled onto their port sides. This collapse, which happened during a fierce storm when the ship was under more stress, released some 200 tons of lard (originally in wooden barrels) from her now-collapsed holds. The 200 tons of lard was washed ashore at the small fishing village of Johnshaven to the south, and littered the foreshore. On 21 March 1969, the local newspaper, *The Mearns*

Leader, carried the story of the 'Tons of sticky foul-smelling lard' that was clogging the foreshore north and south of Johnshaven. The strange flotsam had first begun flowing into Johnshaven Harbour the previous week, but heavy seas had increased the volume of what was being washed ashore. The remains of 400 barrels, which originally encased the lard, were also found - battered out of shape by the waves.

Right up until the 1980s, from time-to-time after a storm, large barrel-shaped pieces of lard (the wooden barrel itself rotted away) would be washed up on the shore. Scraping off the rancid fat, some canny locals would heat up the good fat and use it for cooking, despite its long immersion in the sea. The locals discovered that you had to be careful how you heated the fat, because you occasionally got a German machine-gun bullet in it.

Today, the wreck of the *Taurus* is perhaps one of the finest on the north-east coast of Scotland. The main central section of the wreck remains sitting on her keel, covered in sea life. The bow and stern sections, although intact, have rolled onto their port sides and the holds adjoining the split have collapsed.

MS Taurus.

The wreck has two foredeck cargo hatches and a bridge superstructure – originally five or six levels high – that rises up 10 metres from the seabed. This multi-deck bridge superstructure is one of the highlights of diving the wreck. Large square windows framed in brass (now green with verdigris) still allow views out of the rooms. On the southern side of the wreck (the side which faces towards the large tidal estuary at Montrose), a silt bank has been piled right up to main deck level and (since the wreck illustration was created) has built up to almost the top of the bridge superstructure itself. The port windows now look out into pure mud. The seabed is engulfing this wreck.

Shipwreck – the essentials

Type of wreck	steamship
Nationality	Norwegian
Launched	1935
Dimensions	408.6 ft x 55.3 ft x 25.2 ft
Tonnage	4,767 grt
Date sunk	6 June 1941
Cause of sinking	bombed in enemy air attack
Depth of water	50 metres
Least depth above wreck	39 metres
Position	56° 48.52N, 002° 12.912W

Aft of the bridge, is a collapsed midships cargo hatch. Aft of that, is a second superstructure one deck level high and lined with cabins down either side, each with its own individual sink. This superstructure contains the engine room, hospital, and a galley at the aft-most section. Atop the deckhouse is the pitched roof of the engine room. Divers can enter the engine room through large rectangular skylights and see the massive seven-cylinder engine running fore and aft for about 35 feet. The cavernous engine room drops away into the depths below the level of the seabed outside the wreck, and it too is filling up with silt. Aft of that, are two further cargo hatches holds, with the weather deck having collapsed downwards

The very stern itself, like the fo'c'stle, has cracked and rolled onto its port side. The large non-ferrous propeller is still *in situ*, half-buried in the silt. The steel spoked auxiliary steering helm stands proudly at the stern directly above the rudder, allowing manual turning of the rudder if control from the main bridge was lost.

SS *FRAM*, ABERDOUR BAY, MORAY FIRTH

The 2,491-grt steamship *Fram* was built in Middlesbrough in 1897 for the Danish–Russian Steamship Co. At her launch, she was christened the *Russ*. She was 314.7 ft in length, with a beam of 43 ft. and had a service speed of 9–10 knots.

At first, after her launch, she was put to use carrying cargoes of wood and pulp around the Baltic ports. But in April 1920, the Danish-Russian Steamship Co. and its entire fleet was taken over by another shipping line, Det Forenede Dampskibsselskab, based in Copenhagen, Denmark. Two years later, in October 1922, they sold the *Russ* to a Swedish line, Angfartyg A/B Kjell, based in Kalmar on the Baltic. At this time, she was renamed *Fram*.

Before the *Titanic*, the previous ship with the name *Fram* (built in 1892) was perhaps the most famous ship in the world. She was a radical polar exploration vessel, which had cleverly had her hull constructed to a new design. Before this innovation, ships trapped in polar ice had often been crushed and destroyed by the great pressure of the ice around: think of the famous images of the great British explorer Ernest Shackleton's vessel *Endurance* locked in the ice, crushed and sunk in 1915. The *Fram*'s hull was designed in such a way that if trapped in ice, rather than trying to resist the crush and pressure, her rounded hull would allow her to be squeezed and then rise above the ice. She was the ship that the legendary Norwegian polar explorer Roald Amundsen used in his 1910–12

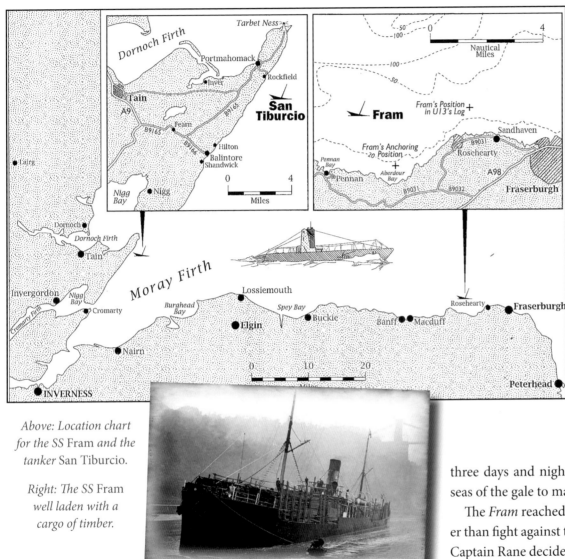

Above: Location chart for the SS Fram *and the tanker* San Tiburcio.

Right: The SS Fram *well laden with a cargo of timber.*

miles short of a food and stores depot. The first *Fram* was left to decay in storage from 1912 to the late 1920s, and whilst she rotted away, the *Russ* was renamed after her – and continued to ply the Baltic ports.

By the time World War II erupted across Europe, the *Fram* – with 43 years of sea time beneath her belt – was already an old lady of the sea. Her captain, Sven Erik Rane, was vastly experienced. He had gone to a life at sea as long ago as 1900 and had been captain of the *Fram* for 15 years before she was went to the bottom.

In January 1940, the *Fram* set out in ballast on a voyage from Stockholm to Hartlepool, Cleveland (just to the south of Newcastle upon Tyne). Her holds were full of boulders to give her some stability until she picked up her cargo in Cleveland. She left the Baltic and passed through the Kattegat: the narrow stretch of water that separates Denmark on the south of the Channel from Norway and Sweden to the north. She entered the North Sea, where she ran into a severe south-easterly gale. It took her three days and nights fighting against the snowstorms and mountainous seas of the gale to make the crossing to Scotland.

The *Fram* reached the north-east tip of Scotland on 31 January and rather than fight against the south-easterly gale down the east coast of Scotland, Captain Rane decided to seek shelter in the lee of the southern Moray Firth coastline. Intent on letting the gale blow itself out before proceeding with his voyage, he took the *Fram* seven miles west from Fraserburgh along the north-east tip of Scotland and anchored her fairly close to the shore in Aberdour Bay, just to the west of the small fishing village of Rosehearty. Here,

expedition, when he became the first man to reach the South Pole. In doing so, he beat the British explorer Captain Robert Falcon Scott, who, caught in a fierce blizzard, perished with his team in their tent just 11

© Rod Macdonald

The wreck of the stern section of SS Fram, *off Pennan.*

138

the land to the south would shelter her from the south-easterly wind, and being anchored inshore, the waves would have little time to build up.

As midnight on the 31 January passed and 1 February dawned, one solitary crewman was on anchor watch to ensure she didn't drag her anchor. The rest of the crew were asleep below decks. The apparently peaceful scene however was an illusion – for the small German coastal submarine *U-13* was on the prowl: on the surface and under cover of darkness, she was scouting for prey. Lookouts on her conning tower spotted the lone silhouette of the *Fram* at anchor – and *U-13* manoeuvered into a firing position.

At 00.43 a.m., *U-13* fired a single torpedo, which struck the *Fram* amidships. The force of the explosion was catastrophic. It wreaked havoc in the bridge, chartroom and central accommodation area and the funnel was destroyed. The ship's lifeboats were also destroyed, along with two of her dinghies. The *Fram* split in two almost immediately and both sections started to settle into the water.

The crew had mostly been asleep below decks. One minute they were warm in their bunks, the next they were pitched from them by the force of the explosion. All power and electricity was immediately destroyed and below decks, all the lit corridors, cabins and rooms were suddenly thrown into darkness. Jolted from the warmth of sleep, the crew instantly found themselves far out at sea, struggling for their lives in the freezing winter night as their ship sank around them.

As the *Fram* broke into two sections, so the crew found themselves divided up between those sections. The bow section, held in position by her anchor, was rapidly filling with water and settling down. The stern section, now free from the bow and its anchor chain, started to drift before the strong south-easterly wind and prevailing seas. It would remain afloat for another 30 minutes and manage to drift before the wind for 1.5 miles to the west.

Eleven of the crew found themselves on the bow section, and with the lifeboats destroyed, they frantically fought to free the life rafts. The bow section sank so quickly that, sadly, the suction dragged some of the crew

and the rafts under. However, one raft popped to the surface, and seven of the crew – some still in pyjamas – managed to board it. The same strong south-easterly winds that had driven the water-filled stern section for 1.5 miles quickly carried the light bow-raft away from the land and out into the open bleak expanses of a stormy night on the Moray Firth.

After six or seven hours freezing in the exposed raft, when dawn came the survivors could see the land in the distance – they realised they were a tiny speck of humanity in the vast expanse of the Moray Firth but would they be spotted? At first, as the hours went past, no help came – but then at about 1 p.m., their luck changed. The crew on the Aberdeen trawler *Viking Deeps*, fishing in the area, spotted the small raft drifting about ten miles offshore north of Troup Head. When they approached the raft, the crew were so numbed with cold that they were unable to climb aboard the trawler. They had to be rolled aboard on wires.

The *Viking Deeps* took the bow-raft survivors to the nearby town of Macduff, and on arrival they were taken to the local hospital. They soon relayed their story of the night-time U-boat attack and of the raft that got away from the stern section. They told how their ration of water on the raft had been frozen and how they had licked snow off their clothes and faces to quench their thirst. Waves had continuously broken over the small raft and they spent most of the night sitting waist deep in the water. To keep their spirits up they had sang most of the night – mostly Swedish children's psalms. On a few occasions they saw other ships in the distance but had no means of attracting their attention. They were an invisible speck in the darkness.

At 8.35 a.m. the next morning, 2 February (the second day after the sinking), as a result of the bow-raft crew's information, the Fraserburgh lifeboat was called out to go to the assistance of any further survivors at the scene. A search was made of the area but no trace of the other raft could be found.

But against the odds, the crew on the stern-raft were still alive, drifting far out into the Moray Firth. In their small water-filled raft, they had endured the

Shipwreck – the essentials

Type of wreck	steamship
Nationality	Swedish
Launched	1897
Dimensions	314.7 ft x 43 ft x 20.5 ft
Tonnage	2,491 grt
Date sunk	1 February 1940
Cause of sinking	torpedoed by *U-13*
Depth of water	bow section: 38 metres
	stern section: 50 metres
Least depth above wreck	bow section: 38 metres
	stern section: 44 metres – main deck
Position	bow: 57° 42.097N, 002° 10.584W
	stern: 57 42.76N, 02 13.492W

for the film *Local Hero*. It has been dived since the 1970s and lies on its starboard side in 50 metres of water. When portholes were recovered from the wreck in the 1980's they were found to have pieces of WWII Swedish newspapers jammed in where the opening circular glass section meets the rim – being used to help seal leaky portholes. The stern section of the hull is largely intact, although all trace of any superstructure is gone. Her unusual square-bladed propeller still sits in place.

Forward from the stern section, the wreck has collapsed and the propeller shaft leads forward through the remains of her aft holds to the engine room, where a small, pitched roof can be seen. Not far away, there is a black-and-white tiled floor. Forward from the engine room, the hull breaks up at the boiler room, with condensers having spilled their copper piping into a tangled mess. The hull ends abruptly where it sheared off from the bow section in the attack.

Both the bow and stern sections lie in an area known for its clear underwater visibility – it is common to get visibility of 20 metres and be able to take in large sections of the wreck at one time.

THE TANKER *SAN TIBURCIO*, TARBAT NESS, MORAY FIRTH

The *San Tiburcio* was an 8,266-dwt British steam-driven tanker built for the famous Eagle Fleet in 1921 by Standard Ship Building Corporation at Shooters Island, New York. She was launched on 29 January 1921 and measured 413 ft in length, with a beam of 53.4 ft and a draft of 31.1 ft.

The tankers of the early part of the 20th century were of simple construction: basically a long, steel box divided into a series of compartments. The forward spaces were designed to carry water and dry cargo, such as oil in drums and spare bunkers. The after spaces held water, coalbunkers and cargo pumps, with the boilers and engine at the very stern. This arrangement minimized the risk of fire, by keeping the boilers, engine and machinery as far away as possible from the volatile cargo.

Between the forward and after spaces, the rest of the ship was divided

night of the sinking itself, the following brutally cold, bleak winter's day, and then a second night at sea. It was a staggering 36 hours after the sinking before a patrolling British aircraft spotted the raft. Despite their two-night ordeal, ten hardy souls had survived exposure, hypothermia and the cruel sea.

In total, ten of the crew of the *Fram* died, including the captain and stewards.

On 31 May 1940, just four months after sinking the *Fram*, the Royal Navy sloop *HMS Weston* detected *U-13* off Lowestoft, north of Newcastle upon Tyne. She was depth-charged and sent to the bottom.

Today, the bow-to-midships section of the *Fram* still sits in Aberdour Bay in about 38 metres of water – only being located by divers in the 1990s. It is well flattened by the pounding seas, and for many years just the very tip of the fo'c'stle was intact – pointing directly upwards. That small section has now collapsed and the area is a general debris field.

The stern section lies 1.5 miles away off Pennan – famous as the setting

The wreck of the tanker San Tiburcio – *she broke in two after striking a mine.*

© Rod Macdonald

into cargo tanks – with often as many as 33 individual compartments. Each cargo tank could be filled and emptied independently, enabling different types of oil to be loaded into separate tanks and subsequently discharged without being contaminated. This subdivision gave tankers exceptional strength and stability, and it was found that tankers could stay afloat despite more than one large hole being blasted open beneath the waterline.

Numerous valves linked every tank to a system of pipelines inside the ship that led to the ship's pumps. From here, another set of pipelines led to the tanker's decks, where they were conveniently located for connecting to shore pipelines for loading and discharging. The Pump Room was usually a small separate deckhouse situated in front of the stern superstructure. The ship's pumps were primarily used for pumping the cargo out of the ship to the shore, and for pumping ballast water in and out. Shore pumps were used for pumping the oil cargo into the ship's tanks.

The *San Tiburcio*'s deck was a continuous weather-deck, penetrated only by small cargo hatches – one for each individual oil tank with a water-tight lid kept sealed. Above the weather-deck, were three superstructures: the fo'c'stle deckhouse; the midships bridge area; and the aftcastle at the stern. These three deckhouses were connected by the 'flying bridge': an aerial walkway that ran along the centre-line of the vessel, about 8 ft above the deck. Because of their strong construction and sub divisions, tankers were allowed to load more deeply than traditional steamships. A fully laden tanker would lie deep in the water and in rough weather, the main deck was continuously swept by waves. The tanker would become a three-island ship, with only its three superstructures visible, connected by the flying bridge.

The Eagle Oil Fleet was founded in 1912 to serve an oil empire created by Weetman Pearson, first Viscount Cowdray, who staked his entire personal fortune and reputation to create an oil empire in Mexico. All the Eagle Fleet tankers – such as *San Tiburcio*, *San Cristobal* and *San Bernardo* – were named after Mexican saints. The *San Tiburcio* herself was built as part of an order for 25 new ships for the Eagle Fleet to be launched between 1921 and 1924 – partly to replace the five tankers sunk during World War I.

The Eagle Fleet tanker San Tiburcio.

The shallow draft of the smaller tankers, such as *San Tiburcio*, allowed them to navigate the shallow channels through the River Plate estuary and reach the shallower ports of the rapidly expanding South American market further up river – where the larger 15,000-grt tankers could not reach.

After 19 years of plying the Mexico/South America trade route, when World War II erupted, the British Ministry of War Transport chartered the *San Tiburcio*. At the end of April 1940, she was sent to Scapa Flow: the Royal Navy main Atlantic base and fleet-anchorage in the Orkney Islands. Here, she was loaded up with 2,193 tons of fuel oil and 12 aeroplane floats, and directed to deliver her cargo to Invergordon in the Cromarty Firth – the sheltered inlet that runs off the larger Moray Firth in the north-east corner of Scotland.

Once loaded, *San Tiburcio* left the sheltered confines of Scapa Flow and headed south, crossing the notorious stretch of water, the Pentland Firth, before running down the north-east tip of Scotland. A trawler escort vessel,

HMS *Leicester City*, accompanied her. But as the *San Tiburcio* hugged the north-east coast and closed on Invergordon, little did her crew know that they were steaming directly into danger. Some three months earlier, on 9 February 1940, the 329-ton Type IIB German mine-laying submarine *U-9*, under the command of Fregatten Kapitän Wolfgang Lüth, had slipped unseen through these waters and deployed her complement of eight contact mines at a depth of 8 metres. This was deep enough to let small vessels, unworthy of an expensive mine, pass overhead: they were intended to catch bigger prey. For three months the mines had lain in wait for such an unsuspecting and worthy victim.

At 10.10 p.m. on the evening of 4 May 1940, the *San Tiburcio* struck one of *U-9*'s mines. The explosion of the mine shattered the usual rhythm of ship-board life and brought the tanker wallowing slowly to a stop, as water flooded into her hull. A tug and the A-class destroyer HMS *Codrington* were sent to her assistance.

If the explosion had happened anywhere else on her hull, her system of watertight compartments might have saved her – but the water rushing into her hull spaces produced a stress right across her weakest point, just aft of the midships bridge superstructure. The hull suddenly gave way and she broke, almost in a clean line, straight across the deck from one side of the hull to the other – as though cut by a knife.

But *San Tiburcio* was not finished yet: her system of watertight compartments managed top keep both sections of the tanker afloat in close proximity for 45 minutes. Miraculously, no one had been injured in the explosion and as she had stayed afloat for so long, all her crew of 40 were able to abandon ship. Her escort, HMS *Leicester City*, picked them all up safely

Both sections of the *San Tiburcio* finally sank into 30–35 metres of water – both settling on an even keel on the sandy seabed almost at right-angles to each other and only about 30 metres apart.

U-9 herself survived for another four years, and took a heavy toll on Allied shipping. She was finally bombed and sunk by Soviet aircraft on the 20 August 1944, at Konstanza in the Black Sea.

Within days of the sinking of the *San Tiburcio*, a green Dhan buoy was laid about 500 yards north-east of the wreck, although given the depth, the wreck was not considered a danger to other surface vessels. The buoy remained in place for 18 years, until removed in May 1958, when presumably any thought of salvaging the wreck had been abandoned. The Royal Navy used explosives to blast the defensive stern gun off the stern section in 1989.

Today, both sections of the hull remain structurally intact, although the superstructures are rotted and collapsing. The straight-stemmed bow itself is a magnificent sight with both anchors still held snug in their hawses. A scour pit in the seabed has been excavated around the bow by the current and this goes well down below the level of the surrounding seabed. Portholes dot around the fo'c'stle.

The main weather deck is punctuated by a number of small oil tank hatches and running fore and aft about 8 ft. off the deck is the remains of the flying bridge. The skeletal remains of the bridge superstructure still holds much of interest. The Pump Room can be found just in front of this superstructure.

Shipwreck – the essentials	
Type of wreck	tanker
Nationality	British
Launched	29 January 1921
Dimensions	413 ft x 53.4 ft x 31.1 ft
Tonnage	8,266 dwt
Date sunk	4 May 1940
Cause of sinking	mine laid by *U-9*
Depth of water	30–35 metres
Least depth above wreck	25 metres
Position	57° 46.34N, 003° 45.32W

Below: The wreck of HMS Pathfinder, the first British naval vessel to be sunk by torpedo from a U-boat in WWI lies with its bow blown off in 68 metres in the Firth of Forth.

Inset: The scout cruiser HMS Pathfinder.

© Rod Macdonald

Another scour pit between the two sections of this wreck has been excavated again dropping far deeper than the surrounding seabed. The stern section weather deck is also studded with oil tank hatches and pipes run everywhere on the deck. The aftcastle superstructure, which housed the boiler room and engine room is the most atmospheric – with man-hole access-ladders leading down into the bowels of the ship.

Each of the two sections individually are large enough to take a whole dive to explore. With the usual visibility in this area, except on the best of days, it is not possible to see one section from the other. However, from time-to-time, divers link both sections with a rope, making it possible to circumnavigate both sections in one dive.

HMS *Pathfinder*, Firth of Forth

HMS *Pathfinder* has the unfortunate distinction of being known as the first ship to be sunk by a torpedo <u>fired</u> from a submarine in warfare. She was not the first ship actually sunk by torpedo – which as history records was the 1,240-ton American Civil War three-masted screw sloop USS *Housatonic*. She was rammed on her starboard side and sunk on 17 February 1864, by a spar torpedo attached to the bow of the primitive Confederate submarine *H.L Hunley*. Once the *Housatonic* had been rammed and the spar torpedo embedded in her hull, the *Hunley* detached the torpedo and retired before the torpedo detonated. The *Hunley* sank with the loss of all hands, for unknown reasons, just shortly afterwards.

HMS *Pathfinder* was built by Cammell Laird in Birkenhead, launched on 16 July 1904 and completed in July 1905. She was the lead ship of the Pathfinder class of four pairs of scout cruisers. She displaced 2,940 tons fully loaded, and was 385 ft long, with a beam of 38 ft 4 in. and a draft of 13 ft 8 in. She could achieve 25.22 knots.

Pathfinder had a 2-inch-thick armour belt covering her engine rooms, but which did not run the full length of the hull. She had a partial armoured deck ranging from 1.5 in. to 5/8 in. thick. In 1911–1912, in the run up to World War I, her original guns (six 6-pounder guns) were replaced by nine more powerful 4-inch guns. She spent the early part of her career with the Atlantic Fleet, after which she was moved to the Channel Fleet, and then to the Home Fleet. As World War I started, she was attached to the 8th Destroyer Flotilla, based at Rosyth, in the Firth of Forth.

At the beginning of September 1914, Otto Hersing, in command of the German submarine *U-21*, entered the Firth of Forth – home of the major British naval base at Rosyth. His raid was detected when his periscope was sighted near the Forth Rail Bridge and the Carlingnose Battery opened fire, without success. Hersing withdrew from the Forth and commenced a patrol in safer waters, from May Island southwards.

On the bright sunny morning of 5 September 1914, Hersing spotted HMS *Pathfinder* heading SSE, followed by elements of the 8th Destroyer Flotilla. At midday, the destroyers altered course back towards May Island, whilst HMS *Pathfinder* continued her patrol to the south.

Later that afternoon, whilst at periscope depth, Hersing spotted *Pathfinder* on her return journey, traveling slowly at about 5 knots to conserve her coal but making herself an easy target. At approximately 3.45 p.m., he gave the command for a single torpedo to be fired.

Vigilant lookouts on *Pathfinder* spotted the torpedo-track heading towards their starboard bow at a range of 2,000 yards. The officer of the watch, Lieutenant-Commander Favell, gave orders for the starboard engine to be put astern and the port engine to be set at full ahead with full helm, in an attempt to turn her bow to starboard as quickly as possible and avoid the torpedo. The attempt to comb the track of the torpedo failed, and the torpedo detonated almost directly beneath the bridge. The torpedo blast may have ignited the cordite charges for *Pathfinder*'s main guns and caused a flash, because there followed a second, massive explosion within the fore section of the ship, as the forward magazine blew up. The foremast and No 1 funnel collapsed and then toppled over the side. The crew, below decks in the forward section, were all killed instantly.

Although the massive explosion in *Pathfinder* happened well within sight of land and should have been seen, her captain, in an effort to attract attention, ordered the stern gun to be fired. The gun mount must have been damaged by the force of the explosion, because after firing a single round, the gun recoiled, and toppled off its mounting. It rolled over the quarterdeck and then went over the stern, taking the gun crew with it.

The stricken ship started to sink quickly by the bow giving insufficient time to lower lifeboats. As the water-filled bow sank into the sea, the stern arose up out of the water. With its structural integrity destroyed and under the strain of the stern section lifting, the bow section suddenly sheared off and plunged to the bottom. A short time later, the stern section also sank below the surface.

Fishing boats from the port of Eyemouth were first to arrive on the scene to assist, but they found only an area littered with debris, fuel oil, clothing, bodies and parts of bodies. The destroyers HMS *Stag* and *Express* had also spotted the plume of smoke from the explosion and headed for the scene. One of the destroyers had an engine problem, shockingly caused by a leg in a sea boot blocking a seawater intake.

The authorities at first attempted to cover up the true cause of the sinking. They feared the affect that knowledge of the loss of such a ship to a U-boat torpedo would have – as it revealed just how vulnerable to torpedo attack British warships were. *Pathfinder* was thus reported, at first, to have been mined. The Admiralty came to an agreement with the Press Bureau, which allowed for the censoring of all reports.

Nevertheless, other newspapers soon published an eyewitness account from an Eyemouth fisherman who had assisted in the rescue and who confirmed rumours that a submarine had been responsible, rather than a mine. The true story eventually came out and the sinking of *Pathfinder* by a submarine made both sides in the conflict aware of the potential vulnerability of large ships to attack by submarines. There were only 18 survivors from her crew.

Today, the wreck of *Pathfinder* sits on an even keel in 68 metres of water in a deep channel of the Forth where the tide continually ebbs and floods. Consequently, although visibility in the shallows above the wreck can be quite good, it is common to find that down on the wreck, there is a lot of silt stirred up in the channel and that visibility is quite poor.

The wreck is a military war grave and great respect must be shown whilst diving it. Small personal items – a brass sextant in the bridge area and brass light cages and lanterns – are strewn about, and all over the wreck are the reminders that this was a warship. Many 4-inch shells litter the site and some of the nine 4-inch main guns themselves can be spotted around the wreck. The stern gun is missing.

The entire bow section from forward of the main bridge support is missing, seemingly cut cleanly off from one side of the hull to the other. It has been located about a mile away.

On the main section of the wreck, at the cut off, the deck collapses downwards towards the seabed. Here, there is an ancient large gauge net lying over parts of it. The Royal Navy draped a net over the wreck just after the sinking to catch any bodies floating free from it and it may be part of that net that remains.

Shipwreck – the essentials	
Type of wreck	Pathfinder class scout cruiser
Nationality	British
Launched	16 July 1904
Dimensions	385 ft x 38.4 ft x 13.8 ft
Displacement	2,940 tons
Date sunk	5 September 1914
Cause of sinking	torpedo from *U-21*
Depth of water	68 metres
Least depth above wreck	55 metres
Position	56 07.09N, 002 10.05W

Pathfinder had a high forward fo'c'stle deck and aft of the skeletal remains of the bridge superstructure, the wreck drops sharply down to the main deck where sections of a long one deck-high superstructure still remain, housing various rooms and the funnel openings. Lifeboat davits are still dotted along either side of the vessel and when the wreck was first dived in the 1990's, some of these still had the remains of their ropes hanging from them. There is a scour pit around the stern that has exposed the starboard side propeller, free section of shaft and A-bracket.

SS MONGOLIAN, FILEY BAY, YORKSHIRE

The Yorkshire coast of England saw a huge number of shipping losses during both world wars of the 20th century. The heavy industries of the major east-coast cities meant that shipping up to Scottish ports and down to London and other east coast ports was prolific. During World War I, small coastal U-boats were specifically tasked to operate around the entrances to these ports, striking at unsuspecting steamships. The *Mongolian* would be a victim of one such U-boat. (During WWII the Northern Mine Barrage of more than 90,000 mines was laid from London to Orkney to try and prevent U-boat attack.)

The 4,838-grt SS *Mongolian* was built for the Allan Line Steamship Co. Ltd of Glasgow, by D. & W. Henderson Ltd, Glasgow, in Partick in 1891. She was a sizeable 400 ft in length, with a beam of 45 ft 2 in. and a depth of hold of 30 ft 6 in. She was built at a time when the transition from sail to steam had not been fully and completely made, and as a consequence, she was fitted out with two towering-masts rising up some 100 ft, the foremast being rigged for sail. She was built with the classic straight stem of her era, with a raised fo'c'stle at the bow.

The *Mongolian* had a long and varied career at sea of 27 years – in a variety of roles and incarnations – before a torpedo from *UC-70* blasted into her and sent her to the bottom of Filey Bay on 21 July 1918, just four months short of the Armistice which halted the fighting.

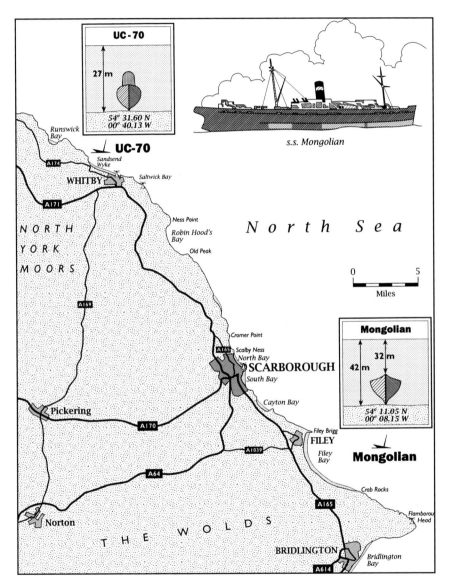

Location chart for SS Mongolian.

The wreck of SS Mongolian lies in the dark depths of Filey Bay, Yorkshire.

© Rod Macdonald

After construction, she was at first put to work on a transatlantic run from Liverpool to Quebec. She often started her journey at Glasgow, before travelling to Liverpool to collect more passengers and then heading out through the North Channel between Ireland and the west coast of Scotland. The main bulk of her passengers were usually emigrants fleeing poverty in Britain for a new life in America or Canada. They were miners, ranchers, farm labourers – men with practical skills needed there, as well as many unaccompanied women with children, travelling to meet husbands who had gone out previously to find employment and settle.

The *Mongolian* tirelessly crossed and re-crossed the Atlantic with its human cargo from 1891 onwards, and was involved in a now-almost-forgotten chapter of British history: the Home Children. In this scheme, more than 100,000 British children were packed off by their parents – driven by poverty – between 1870 and 1930 to work on Canadian farms. They were tagged and shipped in vessels such as the *Mongolian* as a human cargo, bound for farmers in Canada and destined never to see their mothers and fathers again. Travelling in groups of up to 400, with their worldly possessions in small trunks, they travelled to what they thought was a land of plenty. Once ashore, they found themselves arriving on foreign railway platforms with name-tags around their necks, to be met by unknown farmers.

The *Mongolian* was eventually sold to the British Admiralty in 1915. Three years later, in July 1918, she found herself berthed in the northern port of Middlesbrough, being loaded with a general cargo destined for the Italian Government. The first leg of her voyage would take her down the east coast of England to London.

Once laden, she nudged out into the River Tees before moving out into Tees Bay. Moving farther out to sea, she swung to the south, heading for the deeper water of the North Sea. Her scheduled route would take her down the east coast, southwards and a few miles offshore. As she steamed southwards, she was unaware that hidden in the dark, silty waters ahead, *UC-70* was on patrol. Whitby, and then Scarborough, hove into view and passed by on her starboard side.

SS Mongolian *under way in port. Note the foremast rigged for sail.*

UC-70 of the Second Flanders Flotilla, based in Zeebruge, was a small U-boat of just 417 tons and some 49 metres in length. She was fitted with two forward-facing torpedo tubes and one aft-facing tube. These tubes were fitted outside the pressure hull itself: hence the tubes could not be reloaded underwater. Her main role was as a mine-laying submarine – and she carried a formidable cargo of 18 mines, loaded in-dock into six vertical tubes running fore and aft along the forward section of her hull, which allowed them to be deployed in close proximity to each other. *UC-70* was designed to operate in shallow coastal waters, laying minefields across the entrances to enemy ports and coastal shipping lanes. Her torpedo tubes were loaded and ready to use, should any other worthwhile prey cross her path.

The approaching telltale plume of black smoke from the southbound *Mongolian*'s single smoke stack probably first alerted *UC-70* to the possibility of a kill. The slow, old and large profile of the *Mongolian* probably made her an easy target. A torpedo from *UC-70* was loosed and blasted into the *Mongolian*'s port side in the vicinity of her boiler room. In a split second, her hull had been ripped open to the sea and water started to pour into her innards, immediately altering her trim and forcing her engines out of operation. She slewed to a wallowing halt and started to settle into the water. The order to abandon ship was given and the wooden lifeboats were swung out from their davits above her large central superstructure and lowered. As her crew abandoned ship, they knew that many of their shipmates had been lost in the torpedo strike. When a final headcount was made after survivors had been picked up, it was found that 36 of her crew had perished.

UC-70 went on to return safely from her patrol to her base in Zeebruge. The following month, under the command of *Oberleutnant* Karl Dobberstein, she left Zeebruge for yet another patrol in the Whitby area. On 28 August 1918, after successfully sinking the 1,100-ton steamship *Giralda* – and less than three months before the Armistice halted the hostilities – she was sitting on the seabed not far to the north of Filey Bay (ironically, not far from where the wreck of the *Mongolian* now lay), trying to repair damage sustained in a new British minefield. Her commander must not have known that she was leaking oil, which was rising to the surface and marking where she lay hidden.

At 3 p.m., Pilot Lieutenant Arthur Waring of 246 Squadron RAF had taken off in a Blackburn Kangaroo bomber from Seaton Carew, near Hartlepool, with a 920-lb bomb load. Soon afterwards, at 3.30 p.m., he spotted a long track of oil on the shimmering calm sea off Whitby. As he followed the oil slick, it led him to a long, dark silhouette lying stationary on the seabed: the unmistakable shape of a U-boat. Waring turned his Blackburn Kangaroo bomber into an attacking run, dropping a 520-lb bomb at the stationary U-boat – and scoring a hit. The sea frothed with the power of the resulting explosion and more oil was seen rising to the surface. The destroyer HMS *Ouse*, on patrol nearby, saw and heard the explosion and closed in on the scene for the kill, guided by Lieutenant Waring with flares. Once at the scene, HMS *Ouse* dropped ten depth-charges at the centre of the dark silhouette. This attack caused more oil and air to rise up from the depths.

A fortnight later, Royal Navy divers located and entered the U-boat, identifying it as *UC-70*. The U-boat now lay in the silent depths, not far away from one of her victims. Young sailors of both sides had met their end in the cold dark waters of the Yorkshire coast – a haunting irony of how the hunted and the hunter both suffered the same fate, destined to lie in their watery graves so close to each other.

Shipwreck – the essentials	
Type of wreck	steamship
Nationality	British
Launched	1891
Dimensions	400 ft x 45.2 ft
Tonnage	4,838 grt
Date sunk	28 August 1918
Cause of sinking	torpedo from *UC-70*
Depth of water	42 metres
Least depth above wreck	32 metres
Position	54° 11.048N, 000° 08.153W